Penguin Books

the darwin Awards V

A graduate of UC Berkeley with a degree in molecular biology, Wendy Northcutt began collecting the stories that make up the Darwin Awards in 1993 and founded www.DarwinAwards.com soon thereafter.

She is the author of the international bestsellers
The Darwin Awards: Evolution in Action,
The Darwin Awards II: Unnatural Selection,
The Darwin Awards III: Survival of the Fittest,
and *The Darwin Awards IV: Intelligent Design.*

Visit the official Darwin Awards website:
www.DarwinAwards.com

the darwin Awards V

NEXT EVOLUTION

Wendy Northcutt

Penguin Books

PENGUIN BOOKS

Published by the Penguin Group
Penguin Group (Australia)
250 Camberwell Road, Camberwell, Victoria 3124, Australia
(a division of Pearson Australia Group Pty Ltd)
Penguin Group (USA) Inc.
375 Hudson Street, New York, New York 10014, USA
Penguin Group (Canada)
90 Eglinton Avenue East, Suite 700, Toronto, Canada ON M4P 2Y3
(a division of Pearson Penguin Canada Inc.)
Penguin Books Ltd
80 Strand, London WC2R 0RL England
Penguin Ireland
25 St Stephen's Green, Dublin 2, Ireland
(a division of Penguin Books Ltd)
Penguin Books India Pvt Ltd
11 Community Centre, Panchsheel Park, New Delhi – 110 017, India
Penguin Group (NZ)
67 Apollo Drive, Rosedale, North Shore 0632, New Zealand
(a division of Pearson New Zealand Ltd)
Penguin Books (South Africa) (Pty) Ltd
24 Sturdee Avenue, Rosebank, Johannesburg 2196, South Africa

Penguin Books Ltd, Registered Offices: 80 Strand, London, WC2R 0RL, England

First published by Dutton, a member of Penguin Group (USA) Inc., 2008
This edition published by Penguin Group (Australia), 2008

10 9 8 7 6 5 4 3 2 1

Cover design by Cameron Midson © Penguin Group (Australia)
Text design by Daniel Lagin
Illustrations by Peter McDonnell and Jay Ziebarth
Cover photograph by Photolibrary
Printed and bound in Australia by McPherson's Printing Group, Maryborough, Victoria

National Library of Australia
Cataloguing-in-Publication data:

Northcutt, Wendy.
Darwin Awards V next evolution / Wendy Northcutt.
9780143010333 (pbk.)
Includes index.
Stupidity – Anecdotes.
Violent deaths – Humour.
Accident victims – Humour.

081

penguin.com.au

Dedicated to those who kept me sane.

Linux guru Greg Lindahl solved server setbacks and occasionally flicked his long hair my way. Kathleen and Brian De Smet invented the beloved Work Party Barbecue for me.

Renaissance dancers Francis Classe, Matthew Larsen, Crystal Larsen, Rebecca Friedman, impeccable Cynthia Barnes, Carey Cates, Ariane Helou, David Eger & ponytail, Kathy Stormberg, Lee Marshall, Elizabeth Friedman, Leia Mehlman, Molly Thornton, Richard Kimberly, Renée Hollomon, Rachael Lorenz, Trevor Baxter, et cetera.

Dutton big cheese Brian Tart, editor Erika Imranyi, and former editor Mitch Hoffman. Cheerful students Jessica Glickman and Desirée Tonello, playwright Stephen Witkin, artists Peter McDonnell and Jay Ziebarth, legal advisors Michael Cantwell and Henry Kaufman, and as always, the dedicated Slush Pile moderators.

Kenneth M. Hollomon, Renée Menard, witty David Gibson, twirling Lisa Lippincott, Raz Dan, H. Peter Anvin, Suzi Anvin, Barry Eynon, Kevin Haug, multifaceted Chris Kelly, Ildico Stennis, Troy Welch, John Warthog Hawley, Jon Barnard, and dome builders Bob Bushman and Mike Bushman.

Tuesday Night Dinnerclub 🐾 ClanLurkr 🐾 TechShop

"If stupidity got us into this mess, then why can't it get us out?"

—Will Rogers

Contents

from an abandoned factory. Their target: the steel girders that supported the factory roof. . . .

CHAPTER 9: FAQ

INTRODUCTION
ABOUT THE DARWIN AWARDS

"Just think how stupid the average person is,
  and then realize that half of them are even stupider!"

—George Carlin

The Darwin Awards, named in honor of Charles Darwin, salute the improvement of the human genome by honoring those who accidentally remove themselves from it—thereby ensuring that the next generation is descended from one less idiot. We applaud the heroic self-sacrifice of these noble men and women, who gave their all to improve the human race.

Of necessity, this Award is usually bestowed posthumously.

Chapter 9: FAQ tells you all about the rules, our history, and the source of new stories. There you will find answers to philosophical questions, and helpful tips to avoid winning a Darwin Award yourself. Meanwhile, dive into this collection of stories about people who swim in the shallow end of the gene pool.

CHAPTER 1

MISCELLANEOUS MISHAPS

The most inventive Darwin Awards are impossible to shoehorn into a category: Roofs and balconies, elevators, chemicals, helium, river rafts, an ax, a Kevlar vest, a paint gun, vodka, bicycles, tires, and a surfboard! The book begins with a random assortment of mayhem perpetrated by Darwin Award winners and their wannabe cousins, the At Risk Survivors.

Darwin Award WINNER: The Enema Within

Confirmed True by Darwin

21 MAY 2004, TEXAS

Do you really want to know about The Enema Within?

Michael was an alcoholic. And not an ordinary alcoholic, but an alcoholic who liked to take his liquor, well, rectally. His wife said he was addicted to enemas and often used alcohol in this manner. The result was the same: inebriation.

Michael couldn't imbibe alcohol by mouth due to a painful throat ailment, so he elected to receive his favorite beverage via enema. And tonight, he was in for one hell of a party. Two 1.5-liter bottles of sherry, more than a hundred fluid ounces, right up the old address!

"He was addicted to enemas." When the rest of us have had enough, we either stop drinking or pass out. When Michael had had enough (and subsequently passed out), the alcohol remaining in his rectal cavity continued to be absorbed. The next morning, Michael was dead.

The fifty-eight-year-old machine-shop owner did a pretty good job of embalming himself. According to toxicology reports his blood alcohol level was 0.47 percent.

In order to qualify for a Darwin Award a person must remove himself from the gene pool via an "astounding misapplication of judgment." Three liters of sherry up the butt can only be described as astounding. Unsurprisingly, his neighbors said they were surprised to learn of the incident.

Reference: *Houston Chronicle,*
Seattle Post-Intelligencer,
TheAge.com.au, Reuters

Darwin notes: My e-mails reveal that alcohol enemas are far more common than I would have imagined. Apparently the alcohol is absorbed more quickly through the capillary beds of the rectum, a fact exploited by an alarming number of party animals.

Reader Comments:

"Up the hatch."
"Drunk off my ass."
"Rectum? Hell, no, it killed him."
"Takes shit-faced to a whole new level."
"He earned the Award—no ifs, ands, or butts about it."
"This puts a new light on the old saying, 'Up yours, mate!'"
"A drop never touched his lips."
"Coitus alcoholus."
"Bottoms up!"

Darwin Award: Modern Armor

Confirmed True by Darwin

26 AUGUST 2006, LEICESTER, ENGLAND

Darren's death was a mystery. The thirty-three-year-old was found slumped over in the hallway of his house, bleeding from stab wounds to his chest. Police initially assumed that an assailant had attacked him, but they could find no supporting evidence. A year later, the inquest revealed why Darren can stake his claim to a place among the winners of the Darwin Award.

Darren had called a friend, but minutes after he hung up, he rang back to ask for an ambulance. The front door was found ajar, and Darren was discovered lying near a bloodstained lock-knife he had purchased whilst on holiday in Spain. The circumstances of his death were puzzling. Forensics investigators saw no indication of a struggle, and the coroner reported that the stab wounds seemed to be self-inflicted. However, Darren had shown no suicidal tendencies.

His wife, who was on holiday at the time of the incident, cleared up the mystery and revealed why our subject will go down in history as a Darwin Award winner. As she was leaving for the holiday, she remembered Darren wondering whether his new jacket was "stab-proof."

"Unfortunately, he was never able to try out his bulletproof pants."

That's right. Darren decided to find out if his jacket could withstand a knife attack. Did he choose to test his jacket while it was draped over the back of a chair? No, our man thought that the best approach would be to wear the garment and stab himself. Sadly, his armor proved less resistant to a sharp blade than he had hoped.

The coroner reached a verdict of accidental death by "misadventure."

Reference: www.thisisglenfield.com (website defunct after June 2007)

Reader Comment:

"Shanks for nothing."

Darwin Award: Falling in Love

Confirmed True by Darwin

20 JUNE 2007, SOUTH CAROLINA

A passing cabbie found a twenty-one-year-old couple naked and injured in the road an hour before sunrise. The two people died at the nearest hospital without regaining consciousness. Authorities were at a loss to explain what had happened. There were no witnesses, no trace of clothing, and no wrecked cars or motorcycles.

trifecta (pronounced trī-**fek**-tə): a wager on the first three finishers of a race, in the correct order.

Investigators eventually found a clue high on the roof of a nearby building: two sets of neatly folded clothes. Safe sex takes on a whole new meaning when you are perched on the edge of a pyramid-shaped metal roof. There was no sign of foul play (only of foreplay). "It appears as if (they) accidentally fell off the roof," Sergeant Florence McCants said.

This is a true Darwin Award trifecta: *two* people die, *while* in the act of procreation, due to an *astonishingly* poor decision. Bottom line: If you put yourself in a precarious "position" at the edge of a pointy roof, you may well find yourself coming and going at the same time.

Reference: MyrtleBeachOnline.com, *The State* newspaper, WISTV.com, Associated Press, Fox News, WTLX.com, WOAI.com, KNBC.com

Reader Comments:

"Talk about falling for someone. . . ."
"Dammit, I *told* her to hold on."
"Diddler on the Roof."

"Life is pleasant. Death is peaceful.
It's the transition that's troublesome."

—Isaac Asimov

Darwin Award: Weight Lift

Confirmed True by Darwin

27 JULY 2007, GUADALAJARA, MEXICO

Twenty-four-year-old Jessica was working out in the Provincia Hotel's gym when she realized she needed something from the floor below. Instead of picking up the phone, using the intercom, or just walking downstairs, she decided that the open shaft of the industrial lift was the communications device for her.

So Jessica stuck her head into the empty shaft to shout to the people downstairs. And somehow she missed noticing that the elevator was coming up toward her. If the elevator had been going down, one could say that she was in no position to observe the approaching lift. But, leaving aside the stupidity of sticking your head into an elevator shaft, how could she miss the mass of metal inexorably headed her way?

Since an elevator cage and a skull are both solid objects, one had to give. Let's just say the elevator won. Jessica will be missed by her family, but not by the gene pool.

Reference: oem.com.mx and eyewitness account

Reader Comments:

"Talk about a brainless fool!"

"Going up?"

Darwin Award: Pushmi-Pullyu

Confirmed True by Darwin

4 APRIL 2007, GERMANY

Around midnight a forty-nine-year-old man attempted to impress his wife with his unbelievable strength. He climbed over the balcony of their seventh-floor flat, clung to the outside of the parapet, and began a set of pull-ups. After a few pull-ups, which were undoubtedly impressive, his sedentary lifestyle began to take its toll. His muscles lost strength, and he was unable to lift himself back onto the balcony. He eventually fell seven stories (eight if you include the ground floor) and impaled himself

> The **pushmi-pullyu** is a fictional Doctor Dolittle animal with two heads at opposite ends of its body. When it tries to move, both heads pull in opposite directions.

on a thornbush. Ouch! The official verdict placed the blame squarely and pointedly on the macho showmanship of the deceased.

9 OCTOBER 2007, OHIO

The German man is not alone in his efforts to impress a woman. An eighteen-year-old was lured by the siren song of the guardrail onto his girlfriend's eleventh-floor balcony. Attempting to impress the lady, he, too, began a set of pull-ups, only to lose his grip and plummet eleven stories (ten

> **"Attempting to impress the lady, he began a set of pull-ups."**

if you omit the ground floor) to land facedown in the parking lot. The Ohio coroner was more charitable than his German counterpart. This death was ruled accidental.

Reference: presseportal.de, *The Plain Dealer*

Reader Comment:

"Best way to get rid of the unwanted hubby."

Darwin Award: Rock Out

Confirmed True by Darwin

17 NOVEMBER 2006, SINGAPORE

Rock and roll will never die.

Picture a college dorm room. Dirty laundry, sexy posters, food wrappers, textbooks, and in the middle of it all, a sixteen-year-old male rocking out to loud music. A typical student, a typical day. But this particular student, rocking out on his air guitar, was about to "take things too far" according to the coroner's report.

Li Xiao, a student at the Hua Business School, bounced up and down on his bed with such enthusiasm that he rocked himself right out of the third-floor window.

Normally the windows are locked, but students reportedly force the locks so they can sneak a cigarette. Perhaps alluding to Ted Nugent's rock song, the court ruled it a case of "death by misadventure."

Reference: *The Straits Times,* Channel 9 News Australia, Reuters, etc.

Reader Comments:

"Did he dive into an imaginary mosh pit?"
"Air Guitar Disaster"
"Oingo Boingo"

Darwin Award: High on Life

Confirmed True by Darwin

3 JUNE 2006, FLORIDA

Take a deep breath. . . . Two more candidates have thrown themselves into the running for a Darwin Award. The feet of Jason and Sara, both twenty-one, were found protruding from a huge, deflated helium advertising balloon. Jason was a college student, and Sara attended community college, but apparently their education had glossed over the importance of breathing oxygen.

A family member said, "Sara was mischievous, to be honest." The pair pulled down the eight-foot balloon and climbed inside for a breath of helium goodness. Their last words consisted of high-pitched, incoherent giggling, as they slowly passed out and passed into the hereafter.

> When one breathes pure helium, the lack of oxygen in the bloodstream causes a rapid loss of consciousness. Some euthanasia experts advocate the use of helium to painlessly end one's life. At least Sara and Jason went peacefully.

Sheriff's deputies said the two were not victims of foul play. They climbed into the balloon of their own volition, and no drugs or alcohol were involved.

Reference: *The Tampa Tribune, The St. Petersburg Times*, CNN

Darwin Award: The Alchemist

Confirmed True by Darwin

10 DECEMBER 2007, RUSSIA

As a child Sergei promised his grandmother, "I will establish for you the elixir of immortality! I want you to live forever." As an adult we find Sergei sitting in his college biology class, licking potassium cyanide off his palm. He had found that magic elixir! He swallowed poisons daily, to strengthen his body and protect himself from death.

He regularly consumed small quantities of toxic mushrooms, arsenic, and cyanide salts, and urged others to join him. During daring nighttime excursions Sergei often said, "I shall not die. I have swallowed poison for years and today nothing can kill me."

After swallowing the cyanide he began to feel ill and asked his classmates to fetch some water. But instead of drinking plain water, he dissolved the rest of the cyanide powder in it and consumed the solution. Sergei was an intelligent student, interested in chemistry and anatomy. He had earned a gold medal and had been accepted into both the Medical Academy and the Ural State University. But Sergei's scientific premise was flawed.

"I have swallowed poison for years and nothing can kill me."

Instead of immortality he had discovered the elixir of mortality. He went into convulsions, slipped into a coma, and died without regaining consciousness. His father praised Sergei as a gifted chemist who died for the sake of science.

Reference: news.rin.ru, news.mail.ru

Darwin Award: Faithful Flotation

Confirmed True by Darwin

AUGUST 2006, LIBREVILLE, GABON

A related tale from a reader in Palorca, Portugal: "I met an elder villager who once tried to walk on water. He strapped small floaters to his feet. He floated, all right, but upside down, head submerged. He was rescued by the spectators."

During an impassioned sermon a congregation was surprised to hear their thirty-five-year-old pastor insist that one could literally walk on water, if only one had enough faith. His words were big and bold. He extolled the heavenly power possessed by a faithful man with such force that he may well have convinced himself.

Whether or not he believed in his heart, his speech left room for only shame should he leave his own faith untested. Thus, the fiery pastor set out to walk across a major estuary, along the path of a twenty-minute ferry ride. Even though he could not swim.

Lacking the miraculous powers of David Copperfield, let alone Jesus Christ, this ill-fated cleric found only a damp Darwin Award at the end of his chosen path.

Reference: World Net Daily, fr.news.yahoo.com

Reader Comments:

"In faith all things are possible. . . . NOT!"
"If only the TV preachers would give it a try."
"The faithful may drink the water, the foolish will drown in it."
"An idea that didn't float!"

Darwin Award: Whitewater Floaters

Confirmed True by Darwin

5 NOVEMBER 1995, ARKANSAS

Tenacity is often advantageous to an organism. Combine tenacity with a lack of common sense and an excess of bravado, however, and the trait may prove deleterious.

An unprecedented ten inches of rainfall had flooded Arkansas rivers over their banks. Stephan, twenty-seven, thought that this was the perfect time to tackle Big Piney Creek, a challenging whitewater run even at normal water levels. Dressed in overalls and a sweat suit, and notably lacking a life vest, Stephan set out with three friends and two rafts "of the type obtained by sending in Marlboro cigarette packs."

Only a dose of common sense stood between Stephan and glory.

En route to the Big Piney put-in, the four men were stalled at a bridge over Indian Creek. The water was flowing three feet over the bridge, and they could not drive any farther. A crowd of experienced whitewater paddlers had gathered there to pay respectful homage to the freakishly high water. This benevolent group implored the foolhardy party to desist. They warned the men that Indian Creek courses through two miles of dangerous willow jungle before joining Big Piney.

"Only a dose of common sense stood between Stephan and glory."

But the men would not listen to reason. They climbed into their lightweight rafts, put in, and immediately capsized. Undeterred by continuing pleas from experienced paddlers, undaunted by the dunking, the men launched again. They managed to stay on the surface for two hundred yards before capsizing downstream.

At this point one man realized he was fighting a losing battle. He bowed out and hiked back to the bridge. Two other men climbed back into their raft, and Stephan decided to venture onward solo in his raft. A half mile later the flotilla had a close encounter with a tree across the stream, and both rafts capsized.

A search party located Stephan's body later that day.

In the final analysis "these inexperienced and ill-prepared paddlers ignored warnings from a group of obviously knowledgeable paddlers. The absence of a life vest was probably the [second most] significant error." Despite warnings, despite seeing the cold water flowing menacingly over a bridge, and despite capsizing—Stephan chose to tackle this hazardous river. His tenacity was selected against, removing him from the gene pool.

In conclusion, "Warning unprepared floaters can be unproductive, but it is worth a try."

Reference: AmericanWhitewater.org

At Risk Survivor: Mushroom Man

Confirmed True by Darwin

4 NOVEMBER 2007, SPAIN

The warning read, "Ingestion of twenty grams is potentially lethal," but a visitor to the mycological conference in the village of Badajoz disagreed with the official assessment of *Amanita phalloides*, commonly known as the death cap mushroom.

Forty-five-year-old Jesus knew mushrooms. He had spent the past few days collecting and exhibiting mushrooms. He began arguing with conference attendees, and to prove his point he picked up the display specimen and began chewing on half of it. Aghast onlookers begged him to spit it out but he calmly finished chewing, swallowed, and went on to consume the remaining half of the poisonous basidiomycete fungus.

Jesus, clearly under the influence of alcohol, insisted that the next few hours would prove who was right and who was wrong. Indeed they did. An ambulance

Mushrooms evolved toxins as a defense against predators, and *A. phalloides* is the most lethal toadstool of all. The death cap is the culprit behind the majority of mushroom poisoning deaths; its victims may include Roman Emperor Claudius and Holy Roman Emperor Charles VI. Many of its biologically active agents have been isolated. The principal toxin is alpha-amanitin, which damages the liver and kidneys, often fatally. No antidote is known for the toxin, nor for the stupidity of this "mycological expert."

was summoned, and despite heated opposition, a friend finally convinced the amateur mycologist to get into the ambulance.

It was lucky that his friend was persuasive. Once in the hospital Jesus started to show the typical signs of death cap poisoning: bloating, jaundice, and continuous vomiting. He spent two days in the intensive care unit before being transferred to a standard hospital bed.

The mayor of the town paid a visit to the foolhardy mycologist in the hospital. Although the man was aware that his liver showed extremely high levels of

"He is still convinced that the mushroom is harmless."

transaminase, an enzyme produced when the liver has to process toxic substances, he told the mayor that he was still convinced that the mushroom is harmless. Maybe a second try will make him a worthy Darwin nominee.

Reference: *El Mundo* newspaper (Spain), www.20minutos.es

Reader Comment:

"Liver Die."

At Risk Survivor: Splitting Headache
Unconfirmed

SEPTEMBER 2007

Darwin says: "This is my favorite story!"

A man was splitting seasoned wood early one autumn in preparation for the quickly approaching winter. One after another he would drive his sharp ax through a log, then toss the split wood onto the pile. He was making light work of the logs when he came to one with a particularly large diameter.

Feeling overzealous, he decided to split the log anyway. He lined up his shot and brought the ax down dead-center, only to bury the blade deep in the girthy log without splitting it. With a swift action he jerked up on the handle to free the ax for another swing. His doing so made the log scoot forward about a foot before the ax broke free.

> "He was relentlessly determined to split the unsplittable log."

Rather than move the heavy log back into place the man stepped forward a foot to take another swing. The second swing met with the same result as the first, as did the third attempt, the fourth, and so on. In his relentless determination to split the unsplittable the man did not notice that he and the log had traveled some twenty-five feet across the yard and were now positioned beneath the clothesline.

As he brought the ax down for another whack at the log, the ax head caught the clothesline, which acted in the same manner as a bowstring. The ax had barely touched the top of the log when the clothesline reached its maximum draw, propelling the ax head back toward the man at an ungodly velocity. It found its mark right between his eyes.

Fortunately, the blunt side of the ax head made contact, and rather than killing him, it merely collapsed his sinus and fractured his skull. He recovered and learned a very important lesson: Always be aware of your surroundings when hurling a sharp object through the air with great force.

Reference: Eyewitness account by an anonymous informant, who says "I *know* this story to be true because the man of whom I speak . . . was me."

Reader Comments:

"Ax how it's done."
"Talk about an ax-ident . . ."
"Don't ax, don't tell."

At Risk Survivor: Gag Reflex

Unconfirmed

12 AUGUST 2004

A story to make parents shudder . . .

Friends were hanging out in the basement, joking around and playing video games. Matt was irritable that night. He chose to deal with the situation by threat. If certain named people did not stop bothering him, he said as he loaded his Tippmann 98 Custom paintball gun, he would shoot them.

Matt assured everyone that the safety was on, and he would not shoot unless provoked. Yet, oddly, one friend was not reassured. He jumped on Matt and wrestled for the gun. Matt threw him aside, and (as he later explained) to prove the safety was on, he opened his mouth, inserted the barrel of the paintball gun, and pulled the trigger.

His eyes widened as the paintball fired into his throat at three hundred feet per second. He fell to his knees coughing blood but

> A reader named Jason says, "I can confirm that the uvula does not grow back. I had a uvuloplasty, a total removal of the uvula for the dual purposes of opening the airway for sleep apnea patients and reducing or curing snoring." Reader Chris says, "I know from firsthand experience that the uvula does not grow back. When I was twelve, a surgeon got my uvula stuck in the suction tube. His solution was to cut it off. I am twenty-seven now and still no new uvula."

refused to let anyone call an ambulance. Trouble with parents would surely result! Yet his throat was so swollen that he had difficulty breathing.

"He refused to let anyone call an ambulance."

After two hours Matt recovered long enough to kick everyone out and suffer in private. He couldn't eat for three days and couldn't talk for a week. Once he was able to open his mouth, he realized he had blown his uvula clean off. It was gone! And he had no gag reflex either.

His uvula is not yet growing back, but he shows no symptoms of long-term damage. Considering how many people die or are seriously injured by blanks, he was extremely lucky. The best part of the story is that neither his parents nor his doctor and dentist ever found out!

Reference: Eyewitness account by Brandon Burdette

Reader Comments:

"Paintball Gun + Teen Boys = Trip to ER."
"Paint your tonsils."

At Risk Survivor: The Spirit Is Willing

Confirmed True by Darwin

11 DECEMBER 2007, GERMANY

Being frugal can be carried too far! A sixty-four-year-old man returning from holiday in Egypt was carrying two pints of vodka. He ran afoul of security while switching planes at the Nuremberg Airport. Rules now prohibit carrying large quantities of liquid aboard a flight, and the staff was adamant. He could not take that vodka on the plane.

Instead of handing over the alcohol, or paying a fee to check his carry-on luggage, the man quickly quaffed the two pints. That much vodka can easily kill a man! He was soon unable to stand upright.

A doctor was summoned. She determined that he had consumed a potentially life-threatening amount of alcohol and sent him to a local clinic for treatment of alcohol poisoning.

Reference: Associated Press

Reader Comment:

"The spirit is willing, but the flesh is weak."

At Risk Survivor: Head Shot

Unconfirmed

AUGUST 2007, VIRGINIA

Skeet shooters at the Amelia Wildlife Management Area were taken aback when two large black males strode toward the firing line across the open shotgun range, toting a sawed-off Ithaca and a large black box. After twenty minutes of target practice they opened the black box and retrieved a polished Desert Eagle .50 AE handgun.

The other shooters, seeing that the two men had brought a gigantic handgun to a rifle range, began to pack up and leave, praying that the officer who periodically checks the range would make an appearance before someone got hurt.

The shorter man loaded his pistol and began sighting on a can about nine yards downrange. His technique for firing the weapon was straight from a movie. He held the handgun out, with his right elbow twisted ninety degrees to the left. The rifle shooters looked on with horror as the round's tremendous recoil whipped the weapon backward into his open mouth, knocking out several teeth.

Needless to say, one doesn't expect him to survive much longer.

Reference: Anonymous eyewitness account

At Risk Survivor: Storm-Water Surfer

Unconfirmed

JANUARY 2007, AUSTRALIA

When flash floods turned Brisbane streets into raging rivers, a twenty-five-year-old Brisbane man came frightfully close to literally sucking himself down the drain of the evolutionary gene pool.

> **"Never surf on a flooded street."**

This man thought it would be great fun to catch a wave on his surfboard. Fun was fun, until his foot wedged in a storm drain and he was sucked down. After a bumpy and winding three-kilometer ride through the storm sewer, he popped out in a creek, relatively unscathed.

The young man who found the lucky survivor had this advice for those thinking to emulate the surfer's adventure: "Never surf on a flooded street."

Reference: Sky News, Australia

Personal Account: A Slippery Slope

Unconfirmed

1960s, NORFOLK, UK

Norfolk, the small seaside town at the mouth of the river Yare, keeps a modern lifeboat at anchor in the harbour. The old lifeboat shed is nearby. Its cobbled slipway descends at a thirty-degree angle straight into the river. Four hundred yards away the harbour opens into the North Sea. The next stop is the coast of Holland.

> **"We decided it would be a great wheeze to roll inside a discarded tractor tyre."**

I was eight years old and not afflicted by the degree of supervision that kids endure nowadays. That summer a bunch of us decided it would be a great wheeze to take a discarded tractor tyre from the dump and take turns curling up inside it while the others rolled us down the slipway into the river. The name of the game was to struggle out before the tyre reached the water.

This provided several minutes of hysterical fun, until the inevitable happened. All hell broke loose as the lucky winner and the tyre rapidly made their way to open sea. . . . The sight of the big yellow Coast Guard helicopter and its crew saving his ass went some way toward compensating for the pain inflicted upon mine by my dad that evening.

Reference: Anonymous eyewitness account

Personal Account:
Bicycle Chain of Accidents

Unconfirmed

JULY 2000 OR 2001, SOUTH COAST OF ENGLAND

A gripping lesson in Newton's Three Laws of Motion.

This account is a testament to the intelligence of teenagers, who are prone to recklessness—a fact I should have borne in mind. On a Sunday afternoon six years ago, our gang of five had taken it into our brains that, since we live near the sea, it would be fun to play on the cliffs.

We took turns riding our bikes up to the cliff's edge and braking at the last possible moment, the objective being a typical competition between young males. The drop to the water was over one hundred feet. After one boy almost flew off the cliff, we made it "safer" by tying rope around our waists, attached to separate pegs anchored securely in the ground. This, we thought, would avert trouble.

Uh-huh.

One boy's bike squeaked terribly when he braked, and it was getting on everyone's nerves. So he took care of the squeak in an ingenious way: He oiled the brakes. Some of you might already realize that this presents another problem, but we didn't see it.

When it was his turn, he rode up to the cliff with the ironic cry, "Watch this!" Indeed we did watch. We watched him apply the brakes, we watched his expression change to terror, and we watched him disappear from sight as he sailed over the cliff.

The rope did its job and halted his descent. But his rope was longer than the others and suffered the strain of sixty feet of falling teenager, as did the waist around which the rope was tied. The impact of stopping broke several ribs and almost cleaved him in two. Not surprisingly, he fainted.

At the top of the cliff the four remaining kids telephoned for help, but the cliff was so remote that we couldn't get through. Instead of running for help we decided to winch him up ourselves. We set about digging up the peg he was attached to. When it finally came free, there was only one person holding it, and he was pulled over the cliff by the weight of the first boy.

Sensibly, he still had his harness on, but the forty-five-foot drop he endured nearly knocked this boy out. Meanwhile, the extra forty-five feet of rope let the first boy plunge into the ocean, where he unfortunately drowned.

The last three boys on the cliff summoned help from the Coast Guard. Half an hour later a large Sea King helicopter attempted to lift the dangling boy to safety. By this point the knot that tied the rope around the boy's waist had come loose, and he was hanging on for dear life.

Whirling helicopter blades build up a massive amount of static electricity as they beat against the air. Each helicopter therefore carries a cable to ground itself after a flight. As that cable approached the boy, he grabbed for it, heedless of people shouting warnings from the helicopter. When he did grab ahold of the cable, the electric shock blew him against the cliff, and he fell into the sea.

Fortunately, he did not drown. He was airlifted to a hospital, where he made a full recovery.

Six years later I still have the scar on my hand where I touched that earthing cable. I owe my life to the work of the Coast Guard that day. Thank you, Coast Guard, for helping idiots like me stay alive long enough to tell the story to other idiots.

Cheers!

Reference: Eyewitness account by Alexander Anderson (a pseudonym)

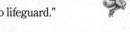

"The problem with the gene pool is that there is no lifeguard."

—Steven Wright

SCIENCE INTERLUDE:
THE WONDERS OF MOSQUITO SPIT
By Michelle Keefer

Mosquitoes—the bane of many a camping trip and barbecue—have been haunting the human race for millennia. But bloodsucking isn't as easy as it seems. These insects rarely get the credit they deserve for their highly specialized methods of overcoming the obstacles of blood feeding. They are easy to dismiss with the flick of a hand, without stopping to think about the amazing ways mosquitoes have evolved to survive on your blood.

Painkillers

You look down and see a fat and happy mosquito feeding on your arm, to which you were completely oblivious a moment before. How did that mosquito suck that much blood from your defenseless arm without you noticing? After all, mosquitoes are basically flying needles, and you can feel a needle prick! A mosquito doesn't want its host to know it is feeding—at best its meal would be interrupted; at worst it would be flattened. So mosquitoes inject painkillers with their saliva when they penetrate the skin, and their victims remain unaware of their piercing proboscises.

Vasodilators

If you've managed to tolerate watching your mosquito sitting there sucking up your precious bodily fluids, then another question may occur to you. "How did she slurp up that much blood so quickly?" Enter another ingenious component of mosquito spit—vasodilators. Generally, an injured blood vessel will contract to decrease blood loss. Obviously, this is not good for the poor little mosquito. The longer it takes her to fill up, the more likely her meal will be interrupted. So she injects vasodilators, similar to nitroglycerin, a commonly prescribed drug that lowers blood pressure. Vasodilators relax and expand blood vessels and permit increased flow, so the mosquito can obtain her meal before your patience runs out and you dismiss her in whichever way you feel most fitting.

Aedes aegypti, the mosquito that transmits the yellow fever virus, injects two vasodilators in its spit, proteins that are similar to a mammalian signaling protein. In blood vessels the injected proteins encourage the release of nitric oxide from the inner lining of blood vessels, which in turn causes the smooth muscle of the vessel wall to relax. Mosquito vasodilators mimic your own proteins, to relax your vessels and continue the flow of tasty blood into the mosquito.

Anticoagulants

A useful ability of blood, as I am sure you are aware, is its capability to clot—a property that threatens the life of a bloodsucking insect! Consider, if you will, the mosquito currently filling up on your arm. Imagine what would happen if your body reacted to the puncture as usual, by activating the blood-clotting system? The mosquito continues to feed . . . until it sucks up a clot, blocking its needlelike proboscis. The "corked" mosquito now has quite a problem on its hands. It is unable to feed. To avoid this perilous predicament mosquitoes inject anticoagulants to keep dinner flowing.

After Mrs. Mosquito settles on your arm, she spends some time probing around for a vessel until she finds one. There are studies on this probing behavior of mosquitoes. You do not feel these shallow punctures because the proboscis is slender enough to slip between the nerve cells.

Our friend *Aedes aegypti* employs a protein that counteracts a specific protein in the coagulation cascade, factor Xa, which activates the fibrous molecule that forms a blood clot. The mosquito protein that puts a stop to clotting is similar to one your own body produces, which maintains the crucial balance between excessive bleeding and excessive clotting by inhibiting factor Xa. The mosquito injects this anticoagulant into your vessel as it starts feeding. When your skin is pierced, your body responds by activating the coagulation cascade. But the mosquito has played its trump card. It has already injected a neutralizing agent that inhibits factor Xa, preventing clot formation by halting the enzymatic cascade.

Immunomodulators

The mosquito has taken her fill and has departed. As you contemplate the mysteries of mosquito spit, you suddenly notice the reason these insects are so loathed. An itchy bump, increasing in size and annoyingness, has emerged on your arm. This allergic reaction is the first sign of your immune system's response to the foreign proteins in your blood vessel from the mosquito spit.

Your body is not at all pleased with those weird proteins injected by the hungry mosquito. An immune response is initiated by the antibodies against mosquito saliva that your body produced the very first time you were bitten. Your cells release a variety of molecules to fight the invaders. Histamines dilate blood vessels to allow immune cells access to the mosquito proteins, causing redness and swelling. Histamine also irritates your nerve endings, resulting in an itch. Leukotrienes recruit immune cells and sustain the allergic reaction, extending the life of that aggravating itchy bump.

Which leads to the most ingenious parts of a mosquito's pharmacological spit cocktail—the immunomodulators. Vasodilators, anticoagulants, and other salivary proteins temporarily suppress your immune system. These immunosuppressants decrease immune cell propagation, histamine secretion, and the number of natural killer cells and macrophages. This benefits the mosquito by delaying the immune response, so the mosquito can finish her meal before you notice the little bloodsucker.

The Perfect Disease Transmitters

Mosquito bites are annoying, but mosquito spit causes no serious harm. However, mosquitoes can transmit West Nile virus, yellow fever, dengue fever, malaria, and other debilitating diseases. As a side effect of suppressing our immune systems, mosquito spit makes it easier for these diseases to infect us. Studies show that mice injected with both pathogen and mosquito saliva have higher infection rates than those injected with pathogen alone, indicating that mosquito saliva does indeed increase the ability of the virus or parasite to infect its host.

The prevention of mosquito-borne diseases is a complex and difficult task. However, some scientists use mosquito spit to their advantage by making vaccines against its proteins! Such a vaccine would decrease the infectivity of the pathogens. Vaccines against proteins in sandfly spit have already been developed to help prevent leishmaniasis. Now scientists are working to develop similar vaccines against mosquito spit to protect against diseases like malaria and West Nile.

So the next time a mosquito decides to nourish her eggs with your precious bodily fluids, take a moment to appreciate the finely tuned system she has evolved to suck your blood. You might also give a nod to the scientists who had to raise mosquitoes (yes, raise mosquitoes!) in order to provide you with this fascinating insight into the Wonders of Mosquito Spit.

Intrigued? Take a closer look at the research:

Champagne, D. E., and J. M. C. Ribeiro, 1994. Sialokinin I and II: Vasodilatory tachykinins from the yellow fever mosquito *Aedes aegypti*. *Proceedings of the National Academy of Sciences USA.* 91: 138–142.

Edwards, J. F., S. Higgs, and B. J. Beaty, 1998. Mosquito feeding-induced enhancement of Cache Valley Virus (Bunyaviridae) infection in mice. *Journal of Med Entomology.* 35: 261–265.

Gillespie, R. D., M. L. Mbow, and R. G. Titus, 2000. The immunomodulatory factors of bloodfeeding arthropod saliva. *Parasite Immunology.* 22: 319–331.

Marquardt, William H. *Biology of Disease Vectors.* 2nd edition. Academic Press, 2004.

Stark, K. R., and A. A. James, 1995. A factor Xa-directed anticoagulant from the salivary glands of the yellow fever mosquito *Aedes aegypti. Experimental Parasitology.* 8(3): 321–331.

Titus, R. G., et al. 2006. The immunomodulatory factors of arthropod saliva and the potential for these factors to serve as vaccine targets to prevent pathogen transmission. *Parasite Immunology.* 28: 131–141.

Wasserman, H. A., S. Singh, and D. E. Champagne, 2004. Saliva of the yellow fever mosquito, *Aedes aegypti,* modulates murine lymphocyte function. *Parasite Immunology.* 26: 295–306.

Michelle Keefer has a bachelor's degree in microbiology from Colorado State University. When she's not in the lab, she enjoys traveling, riding her motorcycle, playing the guitar, and various nerdier pursuits. Michelle currently lives in Fort Collins with—in no particular order—her cat, her Harley, and her boyfriend.

CHAPTER 2

ELECTRICAL EXTINCTIONS

Zap! Electricity has been part of our daily lives for scant generations, not nearly enough time to come to an evolutionary com-
promise with its danger. Kites, electric lines, TV power cords,
stolen copper, and Tasers . . . this shocking subject merits a chapter
of its own. Electricity surrounds us, and the curious human monkey
cannot resist testing the circuits.

Darwin Award: ZAP!

Confirmed True by Darwin

2003, CALIFORNIA

A Los Angeles real estate attorney was skimming leaves from his pool when he noticed a palm frond caught in the power lines. His education had equipped him with sufficient acumen to become a successful litigator, yet he was not shrewd enough to avoid becoming a toasty critter when he reached up with the long metal pole and poked at the palm frond.

Did I mention the power lines?

Our lawyer was, for once, the path of least resistance.

Perhaps as an homage to his litigation skills, his family sued both the utility company and the pool supply store for failure to disclose the danger of poking a metal rod into the power lines.

Reference: *Los Angeles Times*, freerepublic.com,
The True Stella Awards by Randy Cassingham

Reader Comments:

"A true frond."
"Power lien strikes again!"

Darwin Award: Ditched

Confirmed True by Darwin

22 NOVEMBER 2007, NEW YORK

Joe, twenty, was drunkenly driving through Wayne County farmland in upstate New York. With the utmost of inebriated care he steered his car directly into a ditch. Knocked over a power line too. Oops! How could he rescue his car from the ditch without getting a DUI?

The only way out was to steal a nearby farm vehicle and winch the car out himself. So he approached the nearest farmhouse, managed to start a tractor, and motored over to the scene of the crash. With the utmost of inebriated care he then proceeded to drive several tons of metal directly into the downed power line.

Good-bye, Joe.

Hello, Darwin Award.

Reference: democratandchronicle.com

Darwin Award: Copper Kite String

Confirmed True by Darwin

19 MARCH 2006, BELIZE

One string short of a kite.

Benjamin Franklin reputedly discovered that lightning equals electricity when he flew his kite in a lightning storm. However, certain precautions must be taken to avoid sudden electrocution. Kennon, twenty-six, replicated the conditions of Ben Franklin's experiment but without Ben's sensible safety precautions.

Kennon was flying a kite with a short string that he had extended with a length of *thin copper wire*. You see, he was an electrician, and copper wire was just handy. The copper made contact with a high-tension line, sending a "terminal" bolt of electrical lightning sizzling toward the man.

Just bad luck? Not according to Kennon's father, who said his deceased son was an electrician and "should have known better."

Reference: Belize *Reporter*

Reader Comments:

"Let me put it this way, I wouldn't want him wiring my house!"
"An electrifying experience!"
"Shockingly stupid."

At Risk Survivor: Revenge of Mother Love
Unconfirmed

An example of temper overriding thoughts of safety.

Father was watching a soccer cup final on TV with his two sons. As Mum set about her seemingly endless rounds of household chores, she bemoaned Father's lack of interest in washing the car, mowing the lawn, et cetera. Guys, you know the drill.

After ten minutes of ironing and griping she uttered the classic female complaint, "You never pay attention to me!" This met with the usual response from the sofa. "Yeah, in a minute." This was the final straw. She decided to take charge of the situation.

Dramatically, she huffed into the kitchen and returned with a large pair of scissors, stomped loudly around to the back of the TV, grabbed what she *thought* was the cable, and cut through it with one deft movement of the shears. She then made an involuntarily deft movement herself, flying across the room and crashing against the door into a dazed and electri-fried heap.

At that point Father and sons started paying attention to Mum. She survived, and she even laughs about it today. But Father always seems sheepish when the story is told.

"This was the final straw. She decided to take charge."

Reference: Anonymous eyewitness account

At Risk Survivor: Orca Made Me Do It

Confirmed True by Darwin

15 MARCH 2008, WASHINGTON

Zachary, twenty-nine, said he did it to punish the rich white people for the death of the whales and the depletion of the rain forests. He sought revenge by sawing through a sixty-nine-thousand-volt line.

With a tree saw.

On a long metal pole.

Wearing dishwashing gloves for insulation.

He certainly succeeded in making at least one person "suffer just like the whales and trees." Thousands of households experienced a temporary loss of power when he shorted out the power lines. Zachary was found lying on his back, with the gloves partially melted on his hands and his pants burned away from his body.

The unlucky environmental activist was flown to a local hospital and is expected to survive.

Reference: islandguardian.com

At Risk Survivor: Molten Copper Shower

Confirmed True by Darwin

9 FEBRUARY 2008, ENGLAND

Police are hunting for a badly scorched copper thief after finding a hacksaw embedded in an eleven-thousand-volt power cable. The would-be thief also left a lit blowtorch at the scene. He is presumed to be badly charred, and not the brightest bulb in the socket.

"The sheer stupidity of cutting through power cables should be glaringly obvious."

Copper prices have more than doubled in the last four years, sparking a wave of copper thefts across the globe. Thieves targeting copper wire and copper pipes have suffered many fatalities and serious blows.

"The sheer stupidity of cutting through power cables should be glaringly obvious to everyone," said a spokesperson for the power company. "At the very least it would have created an almighty bang and showered him with molten copper."

Reference: uk.reuters.com

Urban Legend: Taser Test

STATUS: Urban Legend

Darwin says: "This story from 2004 is an Urban Legend, according to Snopes.com. Since it's a phenomenal tale of nearly fatal poor judgment, it merits being included among the Darwinian Urban Legends. It is found 'in the wild' as a letter. . . ."

Dear Carl,

Last weekend I was at Larry's Pistol & Pawn looking for a little something special for my wife, Toni. I came across a hundred-thousand-volt pocket Taser. Its disabling effect on an assailant was described as short-lived, with no long-term consequences, but would allow my wife—who would never consider a gun—adequate time to retreat to safety.

WAY TOO COOL!!

Long story short, I bought the device and brought it home. I loaded two AAA batteries and pushed the button. Nothing! I was disappointed, but then I read (yes, read) the instructions. If I pressed the Taser against a metal surface and pushed the button at the same time, I'd see a blue arc of electricity darting back and forth between the prongs, to verify that it was working.

Awesome!!!

I have yet to explain to Toni that new burn spot on the face of her microwave.

There I was, home alone with this new toy, thinking to myself that it couldn't be all that bad with only two AAA batteries, right?

I sat there in my recliner reading the directions, my cat, Gracie, looking on intently, trusting little soul. I got to thinking that I really needed to try this thing out on a flesh-and-blood moving target. I admit I thought about zapping Gracie for a fraction of a second. She is such a sweet cat, but if I was going to give this device to my wife to protect herself against a mugger, I did want some assurance that it would work as advertised. Am I wrong?

So there I sat in shorts and a tank top with my reading glasses perched on the bridge of my nose, directions in one hand and Taser in another. The directions said a one-second burst would shock and disorient your assailant, a two-second burst would cause muscle spasms and a major loss of bodily control, and a three-second burst would purportedly make your assailant flop on the ground like a fish out of water.

A burst longer than three seconds would be a waste of batteries.

I'm sitting there alone, with Gracie looking on, her head cocked to one side as if to say, "Don't do it." But I was reasoning that a one-second burst from such a tiny little device couldn't hurt all that bad. I decided to give myself a one-second burst, just for the heck of it. I touched the prongs to my naked thigh, pushed the button, and . . .

HOLY MOTHER OF GOD! WEAPONS OF MASS DESTRUCTION!

Jesse Ventura ran in through the side door, picked me up from my recliner, and body-slammed us both onto the carpet, over and over and over again. I vaguely recall waking up on my side in the fetal position, tears in my eyes, body soaking wet, tingling legs, nipples on fire, and testicles nowhere to be found.

SON OF A . . . That hurt like HELL!

If you ever feel compelled to "mug" yourself with a Taser, you should know that there is no such thing as a one-second burst when you zap yourself. You will not let go of that Taser until it is dislodged from your hand by your involuntary violent thrashing about on the floor.

A minute or so later (I can't be sure, as time was relative), I collected what wits I had left, sat up, and surveyed the landscape. My bent reading glasses were on the mantel of the fireplace. How did they get there? My triceps, right thigh, and both nipples were still twitching. My face felt like it was shot up with novocaine. My bottom lip weighed eighty-eight pounds. And I'm still looking for my testicles!!

I'm offering a significant reward for their safe return.

Still in shock,
Earl

Reference: Urban Legend

SCIENCE INTERLUDE:
THAT WAS YOUR BRAIN ON DRUGS

By Shelley Batts

You stand at a precipice looking down. Forty feet below is a water-filled quarry. Your friends are urging you to jump. Although your brain knows the water is shallow, those beers you drank have imbued you with false bravery. With a running start and a barbaric yawp you fling yourself into the air, landing on your head and breaking your neck. You're dead. *Game over.*

What did alcohol do to your brain to make your estimation of risk so far off-base?

The Darwin Awards provide ample evidence that humans have no problem shuffling off this mortal coil as a result of plain old bad decisions. But adding mind-addling drugs to the decision-making process further impairs judgment and increases risk-taking behavior, setting the stage for some amusingly lethal acts of stupidity. From jumping into a bear cage while drunk (page 223) to partaking in alcohol enemas (page 4) acute inebriation has been the impetus behind many Darwin Awards.

Alcohol

Besides caffeine, alcohol is the most commonly used legal drug. If you want to be the most popular person at the bar, bring a digital Breathalyzer and test your blood alcohol concentration (BAC) throughout the night. Without fail people will gravitate toward you to measure their own intoxication, often resulting in a contest for the highest BAC. The amount of alcohol circulating in your bloodstream indicates the effects you can expect. BAC levels of 0.03–0.12 percent result in euphoria, which explains why it is a popular social drug. However, as BAC goes up, so does the subjective level of intoxication. Levels of 0.09–0.25 percent induce profound confusion. Levels around 0.35 percent can result in blackout or coma. Levels over 0.4 percent can cause death.

One mechanism of intoxication begins with the metabolism of ethanol into acetaldehyde, which has a depressive effect on the nervous system. Acetaldehyde alters the way that neurotransmitters interact with crucial brain areas. For example, it overstimulates the NMDA pathways in the brain by making receptor

Some people turn bright red when they consume even a little alcohol. A person's ability to eliminate alcohol depends on the enzymatic activity of acetaldehyde dehydrogenase in the liver. Three genes encode this enzyme. A dominant mutation in one of these genes reduces its ability to break down acetaldehyde, resulting in symptoms of acetyladehyde poisoning— a flushed face and increased heart rate and respiration. People with this mutation are less likely to become alcoholics, but more likely to suffer liver damage from overaccumulation of acetaldehyde.

proteins more sensitive to the neurotransmitter glutamate. Evidence suggests that experience-driven activity through NMDA receptors wires up neural circuits. When sufficient alcohol is consumed, NMDA receptors get tired from overuse and shut down, resulting in sluggish thought and movements.

Alcohol consumption also increases the level of a neurotransmitter called GABA that inhibits brain activity. The affected areas are involved in decision making, the formation of memories, and pleasure-seeking behaviors. Alcohol consumption increases GABA production, thus impairing these brain functions.

After a long night of heavy drinking you may have difficulty remembering what happened the night before. Due to acetaldehyde's effects on NMDA and GABA, the areas of the brain responsible for capturing new memories were not working well!

As icing on the cake, alcohol alters how you perceive the world. It blurs vision ("beer goggles") by inducing a sugar-starved state in the visual cortex. It causes vertigo by altering the flow of fluids in the vestibular system, required for proper balance and orientation. Alcohol intoxication also results in delayed response time to environmental stimuli, reducing a person's ability to protect herself from danger or make quick movements when driving.

The end result of excessive alcohol consumption is a person who is dizzy, uncoordinated, and nearly blind; a person whose sluggish brain is unable to form memories properly, and has limited reasoning and judgment skills. In short, a significantly impaired person who is more likely to make that rash plunge over the precipice into shallow water.

Methamphetamine

Somewhere in America someone is cooking a batch of methamphetamine from a recipe including cough medication and match heads. This highly addictive stimulant can be made from cheap household ingredients and has become a scourge of low-income areas.

Meth reaches straight into the pleasure centers of the brain, specifically the mesolimbic reward pathways, causing euphoria, excitement, paranoia, and compulsive behavior. It is a potent psychostimulant, increasing the release of the neurotransmitters dopamine, serotonin, and norepinephrine. This induces the fight-or-flight response. Heart rate, blood sugar, and blood pressure increase; the blood vessels dilate; and energy seems boundless. Such a state can hardly be maintained, and the inevitable crash—low levels of neurotransmitters—is as miserable as the high was pleasurable.

"Meth mouth" refers to the advanced tooth decay often seen in heavy methamphetamine users. Causative factors include dry mouth, drug-induced grinding of the teeth, concomitant use of sugary soft drinks and tobacco, and poor oral hygiene. The condition is so disgusting that images of "meth mouth" have been used in billboard campaigns to discourage methamphetamine use.

Meth is also toxic to neurons. A high level of dopamine causes reactive oxygen molecules to kill brain cells. So in addition to altering short-term brain chemistry, meth also causes long-term brain damage.

In a nutshell, a person using meth is in an irritable, panicked state. Her brain and body have been chemically tricked into defending her from nonexistent mortal danger. This paves the way for erratic and dangerous decisions. Someone wishing to avoid a Darwin Award would be well advised to eschew recipes based on match heads and cough syrup!

Crack Cocaine

Crack cocaine is a highly addictive and impure form of cocaine. Like methamphetamine, crack releases massive amounts of dopamine into the brain, resulting in euphoria. But crack's effect lasts only about fifteen minutes. When dopamine levels spike and plummet, the user's brain function is severely depressed, which motivates the user to find any way to reach that high again. Actions that once were unthinkable, like violent crime, now seem perfectly reasonable if the result is more crack. This is a poor basis for healthy decisions.

Worse yet, crack use depletes the natural production of dopamine, leaving the user increasingly dependent on crack to provide the dopamine needed to function. It is a downward spiral that is difficult to escape. Crack is also notorious for its impurities. Sixty to ninety percent of the street drug is an unpredictable mix of fillers, from baking soda to nail polish remover, that cause a panoply of toxic effects.

Crack and meth both provide an intense high that quickly ropes the user into addiction by depleting the neurotransmitters involved in pleasure and reward. The user must continually seek more and more drugs in order to replace just the normal levels of neurotransmitters, and more yet is required to achieve a high. This dangerous vortex leads to psychosis from brain damage and, eventually, overdose and death.

LSD

LSD or "acid" is chemically known as lysergic acid diethylamide. Albert Hofmann, the scientist who discovered LSD, first accidentally and later intentionally ingested the drug. He experienced extreme visual hallucinations, fear that his neighbor was a witch, and the peculiar notion that his furniture was threatening him. While it

"Warning! Batman Cape Does Not Enable Wearer to Fly."

is safe to say that he didn't accurately perceive reality, the next morning he woke up feeling fine. In the 1960s hippies used LSD to achieve a transcendent mental state. It was considered a promising drug for military interrogations, breakthrough psychotherapy, and as a treatment for childhood autism. However, due to contradictory research results, its potential for abuse and exploration of these uses has been abandoned.

LSD is exceptionally potent. Bioactive doses are smaller than a grain of sand. The mental and physical effects, such as hallucinations, saliva overproduction, and tremors, vary widely from one person to the next and are heavily influenced by the drug user's environment and mindset.

Little is known about the specific biochemical mechanisms underlying LSD's effects. It does alter the activity of many neurotransmitter receptors, including all dopamine receptors and adrenoreceptors, and most serotonin receptors. The psychotropic effects are thought to result from its interaction with the 5-HT(2A) serotonin subtype, but how this interaction produces hallucinations is not known.

It is not unusual for an LSD user to experience dissociation between herself and the outside world. She may think she has superhuman physical or mental powers. This has led to well-known examples of bad decision making, such as being convinced one can fly off a roof. LSD can also induce a highly suggestible state—an effect at the root of the government's military interest in LSD—so a user could be coerced into performing ridiculously dangerous feats she would otherwise never attempt.

Cognitive Enhancers

While some drugs negatively impact our ability to think, others are "nootropics," cognitive enhancers that sharpen attention and focus. The stimulants nicotine and caffeine are well-known legal nootropics. They promote wakefulness, increase focus, and improve coordination via complex chemical interactions with the nervous system. Caffeine and nicotine do have some negative effects such as increased blood pressure and toxicity in high doses. But in reasonable amounts they contribute to *good* decision making.

"Ninety percent of Americans use caffeine daily, and another twenty-five percent smoke cigarettes, making caffeine and nicotine the two most widely used drugs."

One might argue that drug users are primed to make bad decisions, as they already think that intoxication is a good idea. However, there are valid social reasons to use legal intoxicants. There's nothing like relaxing with a cold beer after a long day! But even legal drugs have negative side effects. And while people don't need a lot of extra push to do something stupid, why tempt fate? Next time that jump into shallow water appears reasonable, stop and assess your state of inebriation. The life you save may be your own!

The effect of crack metabolites on heart rate:
jpet.aspetjournals.org/cgi/content/full/307/3/1179

Current research on LSD:
www.maps.org/research/cluster/psilo-lsd/

Shelley Batts is an end-stage neuroscience Ph.D. student at the University of Michigan, a freelance science writer, and a regular contributor to ScienceBlogs. Her work is related to the genetics and cell signaling events occurring in deafness. She enjoys classic Mustangs and teaching parrots to talk.

CHAPTER 3

VEHICLE VICTIMS

We begin with two traffic pranks that turn out badly for the prank-
sters, and continue on with cautionary tales about motorcycles,
trucks, cars, vans, snowmobiles, trains, and a shopping cart. These
stories show that humans still have much to learn when it comes to
coping with the dangers of modern transportation!

Darwin Award: Sudden Stop

Unconfirmed

WISCONSIN

A patrol officer was invited to speak to a driver's education class about safety. Like all such officers he came armed with several cautionary tales, and the irony of this one will stay with you.

In a town down the road, seven college kids decided to raise a little ruckus after a party. They all piled into a pickup—one in the cab and the rest in the back—and drove down deserted back roads, pulling stop signs out of the dirt. Their goal was to get as many stop signs as possible into the truck. Speeding back to the party, the pickup was struck by a delivery vehicle at—you guessed it—an intersection that had, until recently, sported a safety marker.

"Some kids decided to raise a little ruckus."

The six in the back of the truck were killed, and the driver was badly injured. The patrol officer said he would never forget the sight of the dead students sprawled at the wreck, surrounded by twenty-seven stop signs.

Reference: Eyewitness account by Nic

Darwin Award: Merry Pranksters
Unconfirmed

No good prank goes unpunished.

The telephone company was replacing aboveground telephone lines with buried lines in a sparsely populated farming area. Where lines crossed a country road they would dig a trench halfway across, so rural traffic could continue through. After laying the lines, they would fill in the trench and dig a trench on the other side.

One morning local farmers called the sheriff to report a smashed-up pickup. Inside were two ranch hands last seen the previous night, heading home after final call. You see . . .

On their way to the bars the men had decided to play a prank. They stopped their pickup at a trench and moved the flashing warning signs to the good side of the country road. Crime-scene analysis later confirmed that they were the culprits who moved the flashing stands. Investigations also revealed that at the time of the accident they were driving at an excessive speed with an impressive amount of alcohol in their systems.

No crime-scene analysis is capable of determining whether the ranch hands forgot their prank, or chose to see what would happen if they hit that trench at a high rate of speed in the middle of the night.

Reference: Eyewitness account from the archives
of an M.D. with thirty-one years in the ER

Darwin Award: Stop. Look. Listen.

Confirmed True by Darwin

12 SEPTEMBER 2007, FLORIDA

Rare Double Darwin.

A woman wins two concert tickets from a local radio station. She can't believe her luck. The Dave Matthews Band, live! She invites her friend to join her, but they are in for more than a concert experience.

Flash forward to the next morning. The head of operations at the amphitheater looks like hell. Two women were killed the previous night at the concert. He is shocked. Nothing like this has ever happened at the amphitheater.

Flash back to the previous evening, 8:30 P.M. and pouring rain. The show is delayed. Two women leave the venue to escape the rain. They pass multiple free shuttle buses that run directly to the parking lot. Instead, they opt for a shortcut across a seven-lane interstate.

"Free shuttle bus, or mad dash across dangerous territory?" They run a hundred yards through wet grass and jump a six-foot fence that borders the road. Ahead are three lanes of freeway traffic, a hundred-foot median, and another four lanes of traffic. Beyond that is another six-foot fence, the maze of an under-construction garage, and a long hike around a casino.

All in all the "shortcut" to their vehicle covers a distance of half a mile. And the women are in a torrential thunderstorm. Free shuttle bus, or mad dash across dangerous territory?

The head of operations was an eyewitness when the first vehicle struck the women at 8:30 P.M. Oddly, this was in the first lane of traffic, on a straightaway where one can see headlights for miles in either direction. The impact hurled the women farther into traffic, and each was struck by a second car. They did not survive the collisions.

Ironically, one of the women was an "energetic and gifted athlete" who had won two national championships in gymnastics. Physical prowess is no substitute for the homespun maxim:

Stop. Look. Listen. Or tomorrow you'll be missing.

Reference: *The St. Petersburg Times*
and the eyewitness account of Jon Harsanje

Darwin Award: Clotheslined!

Confirmed True by Darwin

13 JANUARY 2008, FLORIDA

Wearing only swim trunks and sneakers, a thirty-seven-year-old man raced his motorcycle toward the Manasota Key drawbridge.

As the bridge began to open, it was clear that he intended to "shoot the gap." Bridge designers had anticipated such lunacy and invented the crossing guard. The closing gates swept him off his Suzuki, over the side of the bridge, into the water, and out of the gene pool. By a twist of fate the motorcycle continued up the ramp and made it across to the other side.

> **"Wearing only swim trunks and sneakers, the man raced toward the gap."**

Darwin notes: My driving instructor was very clear: "Not accidents: crashes. Almost every crash can be prevented by avoiding distractions while driving." He was a wise man.

Reference: *Sarasota Herald-Tribune*

Reader Comment:

"If Evel can do it, *I can too!*"

Darwin Award: Footloose in the Footwell

Confirmed True by Darwin

28 JULY 2006, AUSTRALIA

". . . an accidental shot to the groin." Police wished to question Gareth, thirty-eight, in connection with a stabbing. He evaded that unpleasant business when he drove his car into a power pole. It was initially assumed that he had simply lost control of the vehicle, but Victoria police soon determined that the fatal crash was caused by an accidental shot to the groin. Apparently the deceased had been driving along with a loaded firearm kept handy in the footwell of the car.

Reference: abc.net.au, TheAge.com.au

Darwin Award: Shopping Cart Crash

Confirmed True by Darwin

8 MARCH 2008, FLORIDA

Just because you see it online does not mean it's a good idea. Cameron, eighteen, was joyriding in a shopping cart as he held on to a moving SUV. An eyewitness said, "It's irresponsible behavior, but what do you expect from teenagers?" The car and the cart went over a speed bump and the cart overturned, ejecting its occupant, who was not wearing the cart's little seat belt. Cameron was pronounced dead at the scene.

"It's irresponsible, but what do you expect from teenagers?"

Reference: www.wftv.com

Reader Comment:

"Grocery Basket Follies"

Darwin Award: Organ Donors

Confirmed True by Darwin

3 FEBRUARY 2008, CALIFORNIA

Two dirt bikes, two drivers, two passengers. Zero helmets, zero headlights, and a new moon. Four friends were tearing around in pitch dark on private land, where helmets and lights are not required. Inevitably their bikes collided. The highway patrol said the two couples were killed between 1:30 and 3:30 A.M. in Modesto.

Emergency room workers have a name for people who ride dirt bikes without helmets. They're called "future organ donors," and that is the only career now possible for Thomas, thirty-three; Michael, thirty-three; Kelly, thirty; and Cynthia, twenty-nine.

Reference: SFgate.com, Associated Press

At Risk Survivor: Hook, Line, and Sinker

Unconfirmed

2000, DENMARK

Exhilarated by the freedom of his first driver's license, a young man borrowed a car from his uncle, a car collector, and took his cousin out for a spin.

Denmark winters are usually mild, but this particular year was so cold that the Baltic Sea surrounding the island of Als froze over. When the cousins drove down to the shore, they found

> **"They tested the ice by jumping up and down."**

that Ketting Bay had iced over. They took a quick walk on the ice, tested it by jumping up and down, and decided it was thick enough to drive on.

A few hundred yards offshore they discovered their error. The ice cracked and the car sank. Luckily Ketting Bay is shallow, so the boys suffered no worse than wet pants as they escaped through the car windows. Up to this point their misadventure could be considered a poor estimate.

They looked the half-submerged collectible car over and decided they had better pull it out before Uncle got mad. So they walked back to the farm, found a coil of rope and a strong car, drove back to the beach—and out to the submerged car!

Sploosh.

At this point we would not be wrong to talk about the foolishness of youth.

The boys climbed out of Submerged Car #2, walked back to the farm with sodden pants and chattering teeth, and fetched a farm tractor. They drove back to the beach—out onto the ice—and sank the tractor too!

Submerged Car #1 could be called an accident,

Submerged Car #2 could be called plain daft, but

Submerged Car #3 seems to indicate a genetic error, especially since the boys agreed upon the actions, and they are blood relatives.

Reference: Eyewitness account by Kim "The_Pirate" Christensen, who says, "This happened to a young man who works a few desks away from me."

At Risk Survivor: Mexican Divorce

Unconfirmed

MEXICO

I was traveling in Mexico with my then wife. Like many young hands we were in a VW van equipped with a potty to provide for our fussy American preference for sanitation and privacy.

My wife and I had been quibbling all day, due to the stifling heat and humidity of the sea-level jungle in which we had been camping. We took the road toward Mexico City, hoping that higher elevation would gain us some relief from the tropical heat.

On a switchback road several thousand feet above sea level, my dear wife announced the need to use the convenience and lurched toward the rear of the van. I suggested that she wait until I could pull over, but she was resolute in her determination to attend to matters promptly.

From the back I heard her irritable voice say, "Why's this sodding potty rocking?" I pondered and realized that the potty was under pressure! It had been last used at sea level, and we had gained significant elevation. The bottom of the potty was bowed with pressure, causing the rocking. And, to my good wife's impending grief and mortification, the potty was nearly full.

A beat too late I called back, "Honey don't flush . . . "

I was interrupted by a mighty WHOOSH and a slurpy noise. Then silence. Then a horrible stench, and the unhappy sounds of my dear bride cursing like a Liverpool longshoreman. In the rear-view mirror I saw that the interior of the van was dripping with brown fluid. Since she'd had to face the potty to flush it, and since she hadn't put the lid down, my hapless wife had taken the full blast from the pressurized holding tank. Her skin was brown, and I don't mean suntanned.

Convulsed with laughter that was the proximate cause of our subsequent marital decline, I pulled over. My soon-to-be-ex lady marched down the highway cursing and dripping. When I recovered my composure, I cleaned the van and picked up my luckless hitchhiking wife. Our conversation was limited over the next few days and never regained its former gaiety and charm.

That pressurized potty took us *out of the gene pool.*

Reference: Eyewitness account of an anonymous unfortunate

Reader Comments:

"Oh, fudge."
"Another crappy day."
"If the potty's rockin', don't bother knockin'."
"Getting your own back."

At Risk Survivor: Chivalry Rebuffed

Unconfirmed

MAY 2007, CALIFORNIA

I was taught by my fraternity to believe in human service and always lend a hand, particularly to pretty young women! One afternoon I was drinking beer on the front deck of the Berkeley frat house, enjoying the California sunshine, when I heard the unmistakable *thump-thump, thump-thump* of a flat tire. A Ford SUV pulled up to the curb and two young women hopped out to inspect the damage.

I quickly jumped down from the deck and offered to lend a hand. Perhaps they needed a jack or a spare set of hands? I was rebuffed. "Just because we're women doesn't mean we can't change a tire." So I sat back on the deck to watch the show.

The women retrieved tools and the spare from their vehicle and began to jack up the car. They didn't notice that the car was right against the curb. There was no room to remove the wheel or install the new one. I attempted to step in but was brusquely rebuffed.

Eventually they realized their error and rolled the car forward to the ramp in the curb. Here, again, they didn't take into account the angled edge of the curb, which allowed for drainage. Even fully extended, the jack wasn't tall enough to allow the installation of a fully inflated spare. Again I offered my help. I suggested that they put the jack on a four-by-four block of wood I had handy, to offset the height.

But no! They wanted to change the tire themselves.

The young women found a cinderblock, set the jack on it, jacked up the car, and removed the flat. Here's where the Darwin potential comes in. Until now I had not paid attention to where on the underbody they had positioned the jack. I made the mistake of assuming they knew a jack couldn't go just anywhere. I was proven wrong.

With the jack fully extended and the flat removed, one woman began to put the spare on the studs. If you own an SUV you know these spares aren't lightweight. The woman sat on the curb with her legs extended underneath the SUV, and the wheel hub positioned directly in front of her. Only then did I realize that they had placed the jack on the only "flat" spot of the underbody—the passenger seat floorboard!

Before I could yell, "Get out of there!" the jack tore through the floorboard and dropped the front of the SUV directly on the woman's legs. The hub fell just shy of crushing her unmentionables. To my knowledge she suffered two broken femurs (impressive, given that they're the strongest bones in the human body) but no damage to the procreative parts. Still, she came as close to earning a Darwin Award as I believe a woman can.

Reference: Eyewitness account by Jason Keats

Reader Comments:

"Anything he can do she can do better."
"Now she *can't* wear the pants."

At Risk Survivor: Shattered Ego

Unconfirmed

NEW JERSEY

One warm summer day I was walking along the lake with a childhood friend. We reminisced about youthful summers spent fishing on the lake. A railroad track runs next to the lake. We used to put pebbles and pennies on the train tracks and take cover as the train zoomed by and annihilated the objects.

My friend is a schoolteacher who dabbles in photography, and as we walked, he would take various nature shots. Every fifteen minutes or so a train would fly by. My friend was seized by a creative urge to put stones on the tracks and take a photo as the train ran over them. An action shot, he called it. **"An action shot, he called it."**

I insisted that this was a bad idea, but he proceeded to place several fist-size stones on the rail. I took cover a good hundred yards away as he sat in wait, twenty yards from the tracks. Soon we heard the train approaching. He crouched down and put the camera to his face. As the train flew by, he fell flat on his back!

Exactly what I had thought would happen, happened. The train sent stone shrapnel flying straight toward him, and one piece hit him in the face. I ran to his side. He was spitting out blood and two broken teeth. Despite the look of horror and surprise on his face I couldn't help but laugh. I'd warned him! "At least, did you get the shot?" I asked.

He gave me a look that said he wanted to kill me.

When he developed the film, he found an "action shot," all right. It was a blurred picture of the top of the train and the sky above it, snapped as he fell backward. I suggested posting the photo in his classroom along with a picture of his two broken teeth, and a sign explaining the dangers of playing with trains.

This man, a teacher, is a role model for the next generation!

Reference: Anonymous eyewitness account

At Risk Survivor: Never Change

Confirmed True by Darwin

JANUARY 2006, AUSTRALIA

Who would risk his life for some pocket change? A Darwin Award nominee, of course! A thirty-five-year-old Sydney man lost some change down a storm-water drain. Most sensible people would just let it go, especially as it had been raining. In fact, all sensible people would let it go.

Not our man. He just could not let loose change go. He removed the cover from the sewer, lay down on the road, and stuck his head and upper body down the drain. In this position, fishing around for coins, his lower body was lying across the road.

His financial plans went wrong when a Ford SUV turned the corner. The driver, of course, failed to notice him. One does not expect to see half a person lying on the roadbed. The vehicle's bumper struck the man.

"Most sensible people would just let it go."

Our nominee was rushed to St. Vincent's Hospital in serious condition, with a broken pelvis and internal injuries. Had he been run over by the tire instead of struck by the bumper, police say it is likely he would not have survived.

Loose change is not worth the risk!

Reference: smh.com.au

At Risk Survivor: Bed of Embers

Confirmed True by Darwin

APRIL 2007, TENNESSEE

A twenty-two-year-old man was having a "barbecue moment." Luke's friends needed charcoal embers, and he had the means to deliver, that means being his trusty 1978 Chevrolet pickup truck. So he put his burning barbecue grill in the bed of the truck and set off down the road.

"Obviously, we would urge people not to drive with burning grills in their vehicles," Sheriff's Office spokesman Ted Denny said later. The trouble was, the hot grill was not the only item in the bed of the pickup.

Hot charcoal, meet propane tank.

The propane tank exploded and the Chevy was engulfed in flames. But Luke was lucky. Due to the quick response of emergency crews the conflagration was extinguished. Luke escaped with burns to his lower legs, burns that will no doubt leave scars to remind him that few barbecue emergencies are worth the risk.

"We urge people not to drive with burning grills in their vehicles."

Reference: TheLeafChronicle.com

Reader Comment:

"Bed of Embers"

"I do not approve of anything that tampers with natural ignorance. Ignorance is like a delicate, exotic fruit; touch it
and the bloom is gone."

—Lady Bracknell, in Oscar Wilde's
The Importance of Being Ernest

At Risk Survivor: RoboCop

Unconfirmed

FEBRUARY 2005, CANADA

Canadian winter nights are long and usually quiet, but one exception was the night Constable Morgan responded to a drunk driver
call. He caught up to the errant driver and fell in behind in order to
establish the commission of the crime. In a short distance the
driver missed a curve and slid into a snowbank. Morgan switched
on his lights, stopped his patrol unit, and approached the driver's
door.

The driver decided to flee. His tires, mired in the snow, spun
wildly but the car went nowhere. Constable Morgan thought he
would have a little fun. He began running in place alongside the
driver's window. The speedometer read 100 kph. The driver was
surprised to see the constable keeping up with his car.

Constable Morgan broke the window glass with his flashlight
and ordered, "Pull over!" The driver's response? He jammed the
pedal to the metal!

The car's speedometer reached 175 kph, yet astonishingly, the
constable was keeping pace and ordering the driver to stop. Finally,
convinced he was never going to outrun the fleet-footed officer, the
drunk man let off the gas, turned the wheel, and brought his car to
a "stop." The constable escorted the man to his patrol vehicle, which
had magically followed the two on their mad dash across the snow-
covered tundra.

The man was charged with DWI, speeding, and failing to yield to a policeman. Brought before the judge for arraignment, the man, who had not quite regained his wits, saluted the incredible athletic prowess of the local officers.

Reference: Canadian L.E. Bulletin, February 2005

"If some Power the gift would give us,
 To see ourselves as others see us!
 It would from many a blunder free us,
 And foolish notion."

—Robert Burns

At Risk Survivor: Hurdles

Unconfirmed

2004, UK

I met James at a poetry event in a London café. He was a talented poet and semiprofessional footballer who referred to himself as an unpaid condom advertisement—take one look at him and you'll never have kids, just in case. One day, James limped in. Naturally, I asked what had happened. The resulting account had me in stitches for a good long while.

James had been preparing to cross the road. In a sensible fashion he looked both ways before starting to cross, but he failed to notice a car pulling out a bit up the road. Seeing this car heading toward him at a low speed, James realized he had to get out of the way.

Most people would make a dash for the other side of the road or take a few steps back. However, James's brain cells were out to lunch. The cells that were still on duty in his brain told him that the best way to avoid being struck was to *jump over the car*. He cleared the bumper and landed on his feet on the hood of the car, which continued to move forward at a slow speed. James lost his balance and fell on all fours, severely bruising both knees. He then fell off the car entirely, and the back wheel ran over his foot. Luckily nothing was broken.

His doctor said that if he'd tried hurdling a car that was moving at the speed limit (thirty mph) he would have been killed or seriously injured. Needless to say he promised to stop trying to do hurdles over cars. He certainly gave himself a good reason for his new nickname!

"Hurdles."

Reference: Anonymous eyewitness account

"Human beings can always be counted on to assert with vigor their God-given right to be stupid."

—Dean Koontz, *False Memory*

At Risk Survivor: Brothers Well-Met

Confirmed True by Darwin

OCTOBER 2006, MAINE

Could it be genetic?

Two brothers, seventeen and eighteen, were conversing on their cell phones when the vehicles they were driving met in a head-on collision. Nobody died, but both were injured. The two young men were not even wearing seat belts! The innocent victims were two totaled cars: a 1994 Jeep Cherokee and a 1998 Ford pickup.

Darwin kindly asks her readers to turn off those cell phones! Many times that erratic driver we pass has a phone in his ear. YOU are just as erratic when you are on that phone. For your own safety, and for the safety of those around you, HANG UP!

Reference: Lewiston *Sun Journal*

SCIENCE INTERLUDE: FLOWER POWER

By Steven "DarkSyde" Andrew

A few hundred years ago a new fad swept through the privileged ranks of European aristocracy. It was a substance refined from an enigmatic plant brought back from the New World. Hailed as a godsend by some, more recent experience has shown that long-term consumption can lead to erratic behavior, serious weight fluctuations, and systemic organ failure. Even first-time users can, although rarely, fall victim to fatal cardiopulmonary shock. But it is not all bad. I must confess, on my first date with my future wife, she and I both indulged. The mysterious extract soon worked its neurotransmitter magic. We gazed enraptured into each other's now-blazing eyes, and we fell madly in love.

If you travel back to the opening days of the Cretaceous Period, you are well advised to watch your step. Saurian monsters abound. Hungry eyes watch from ambush. Hordes of tiny ratlike mammals slumber by day in fur-lined burrows, emerging to feed at dusk. Aside from running afoul of a carnivorous titan, you must be careful of the little critters as well. Tread on the wrong lair and you might crush dear old Great-to-the-Zillionth Grandpa in his sleep, wiping out the entire human race and giving rise to the dreaded Grandfather Paradox. With so much to worry about, it is easy to miss the most important new organism to arise in ages, standing low in the tangled bank at the steamy water's edge.

It is the world's first blossom.

The little pockets of flowers were unobtrusive in a world ruled by colossal carnivorous monsters. But the small flowering shoots had already struck a partnership with the most successful animal taxon on earth, the insects, and would soon team up with the rest of the animal kingdom. In its own vegetable way, the flower was poised to take over the world.

Botanists classify so-called higher plants, meaning those with roots, veins, and leafy structures, into two main groups: angiosperms and gymnosperms. Flowering plants are angiosperms. Conifers, which produce the familiar pinecone, are an example of gymnosperms. Both produce seeds. However, the seeds of angiosperms are surrounded by a fleshy vessel, or an *angio* in Latin, forming an often tasty wrapper. The seeds of gymnosperms lack an equivalent structure and thus are "naked," or in Latin, *gymno*.

The origin of flowering plants is a hotly debated topic. Some say there is indirect evidence for a possible ancestor over two hundred million years ago. But the oldest unambiguous fossil evidence for a flowering plant is found in China and dates to about 125 million years ago. It was named *Archaefructus sinensis*, "ancient Chinese fruit."

Regardless of when they first evolved, plants had hit on an ingenious survival strategy. Rather than playing an inadvertent role in the mandibles, jaws, and gullets of ancient insects, they created a sort of organic peace offering, free for the taking. Pollen and sweet nectar was given as payoff for cross-fertilizing the new angiosperms. The flower blossom itself likely evolved as a visual transponder beacon. The blooms even developed secret patterns invisible to the eyes of vertebrates, flashing rings and other enticing patterns in ultraviolet wavelengths to wave in their insect couriers.

By the Middle Cretaceous, some ninety million years ago, birds were probably in on the act, recruited by flowers to carry plant pollen in their feathers and seeds in their stomachs. They flew across the young and growing Atlantic Ocean to every island and continent. Flowers of all kinds evolved, each in elegant resonance to the needs and desires of their local animal partners. By the Late Cretaceous, twenty million years later, the luxuriant emerald-green world of the dinosaurs had been adorned with bright blossoms and sweet scents.

> Research shows that flower fragrances travel only one-third as far today as they did in less-polluted years.

After dinosaurs disappeared sixty-five million years ago, plant-munching mammals rose to prominence, and flowering plants came up with their next smash hits: fruits and grasses. Citrus fruits in particular, of the group *Rutaceae*, are a favorite of tree-dwelling animals. The animals eat the fruity prize; the seeds are safely transported all over the jungle and then deposited in a steaming pile of rich animal fertilizer. *Liliopsida,* an angiosperm better known as grass, appears widely in the fossil record in the Eocene. By thirty million years ago grasses dominated the flat savanna and provided food for the largest mammals ever to walk the earth.

Over the next twenty-five million years a few of these hardy flowering grasses evolved into the forerunners of modern cereal grains:

wheat, corn, and rice. Those three grains account for over half the calories in the modern human diet. A whopping five trillion calories of cereal are consumed each day, and two trillion more in the form of tubers, vegetables and vegetable oil, fruits, syrups, and other sugars made from flowering plants. Added to that, every pound of meat we eat conservatively represents thousands of calories of commercial cereals and wild grasses.

The Plant Kingdom could not have supported the kinds and numbers of animals it does today before the advent of flowering plants. And even with the sweet fruits and toothsome grains they offer, artificial selection was required, operating over millennia on hundreds of angiosperm species, so that humans can harvest the amount of food we currently eat.

Quite literally, human beings are flower-powered.

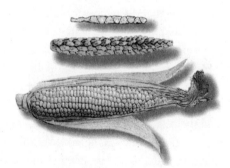

Teosinte (top) began as a single stalk of kernels, each enclosed in its own individual husk. Over time artificial selection produced strains with large kernels and softer husks, until we can recognize the first corncobs (center). Modern corn (bottom) is a mutant version so freakishly large it cannot survive or reproduce without human cultivation and care. Illustration by Karen Wehrstein.

How is all this ancient flowery history known or suspected? Some is educated guesswork. But much of it falls under the purview of paleobotany and palynology, the study of ancient pollen. Most small plants don't lend themselves to fossilization. But plant pollen is tough and fossilizes well. Particular groups of plants can often be distinguished by their pollen. Thanks to the painstaking dedication of thousands of botanists over the years, we have developed a robust database of ancient pollens, tracing the evolutionary radiation of angiosperms onto the global stage.

Of course, the flowering plants could never fully trust their new animal partners. Given half a chance the animals would gobble down the whole plant: fruit, nut, flower, leaf, stem, and root. Evolution quickly produced critters that did exactly that. The plants responded by incorporating substances that give the offending critter a stomachache or worse if it eats the wrong part at the wrong time.

Many of our early medicines and modern drugs come from such defenses. The plant chemicals are bioactive by definition, because they are meant to affect the biology of the animal that eats them. Quinine from tree bark, caffeine from the coffee bean, narcotic painkillers from the opium poppy, and aspirin from the willow tree are substances that don't pose quite as much danger to us as they do to insects and their ilk. Unlike the bugs', our bodies come complete with sophisticated, factory-installed detoxification systems. In fact, for humans, the effects of some of those natural insecticides are downright addictive.

Which brings us back to that first date with my future wife and the highly habit-forming, brain-altering substance we ingested at the dawn of the new millennium. The source was an enigmatic flowering plant found in the New World. The substance it produces is sublime. Yet we broke no drug laws. It was first used in a crude form thousands of years ago by Native Americans in what is now called Central America. The Aztecs called it *xo-co-latl*. But we know it today as chocolate.

Cretaceous dating:

Ji, Q., H. Li, L. M. Bowe, Y. Liu, and D. W. Taylor, 2004. Early Cretaceous *Archae-fructus eoflora* sp. nov. with bisexual flowers from Beipiao, Western Liaoning, China. PDF (3.11 MiB). *Acta Geologica Sinica*. 78(4): 883–896.

Steven "DarkSyde" Andrew is a freelance science writer and contributing editor to the popular progressive weblog Daily Kos. He lives in Florida near the Kennedy Space Center with his wife, Mrs. "DS," a dog named Darwin, and a cat named Kali.

CHAPTER 4

MEDICAL MALADIES

Treatments, injections, bullet wounds, and such populate these eye-witness accounts from medical professionals present at the aftermath of astoundingly stupid decisions. Due to patient confidentiality, most are unconfirmed. But these stories are all plausible . . . and mind-bogglingly ludicrous!

Darwin Award: Not a Shred of Sense
Unconfirmed

The ambulance responded to a frantic call concerning a neighbor's trip through an industrial tree shredder. It seems the individual had decided to prune his own trees rather than hire a professional.

"To save time— those fateful words." Why not? After all, the local shop rented shredders that could make quick work of yard debris, including tree limbs up to eight inches in diameter.

To save time (those fateful words) the neighbor had placed the shredder at the base of a great oak tree, where he could drop branches directly into the hopper. He intended to cut off the top third of the oak, which had been killed by lightning.

With the shredder running wide open, the neighbor climbed his ladder to the first tree branch, stepped off the ladder, slipped—and fell. The paramedics found him very dead, half in and half out of the hopper, one leg shredded to the hip.

Not married, no kids, removed self from the gene pool.

Reference: Eyewitness account of an M.D. who practiced emergency medicine for thirty years

Darwin Award: Stubbed Out

Confirmed True by Darwin

17 APRIL 2006, ENGLAND

There's always someone who thinks good advice doesn't apply to him. For example, if a doctor advises that you are going to be covered with a flammable medical treatment, most people would take this advice on board and not strike a match until the flammable material has been removed.

Philip was in the hospital to treat a skin disease, said treatment consisting of being smeared in paraffin-based cream. Philip was warned that the cream could ignite, so he definitely should NOT smoke. However, Philip, sixty, knew better than his doctor. And he just had to have another cigarette.

Smoking was not permitted on the ward, but Philip took this setback in stride and sneaked out onto a fire escape. Once he was hidden, he lit up . . . inhaled . . . and peace descended as he got his nicotine fix. It was only after he finished his cigarette, at the moment he ground out the butt with his heel, that things went downhill.

The paraffin cream had been absorbed by his clothing. As his heel touched the butt, fumes from his pajamas ignited. The resulting inferno "cremated" his skin condition and left first-degree burns on much of his body. Despite excellent treatment he died in intensive care.

Using the Darwin checklist (criteria outlined on pages 252–254):

1. Reproduction—he may already have children, but he won't have more.
2. Excellence—this one I'll remember!
3. Self-selection—he was warned that paraffin and smoking don't mix.
4. Maturity—at sixty he was old enough.
5. Veracity—major UK news carriers covered the story.

This ticks all the boxes, and though one feels sorry for the family, his death serves as a warning to others. If a doctor tells you not to smoke, there's a very good reason.

Reference: *The Mirror, Yorkshire Today, The Guardian*

Reader Comments:

"Up in Smoke"
"You Light Up My Life"
"Another smoker goes down in flames."
"He suddenly had this burning desire for a smoke."
"Dying for a cigarette."

Darwin Award: Going to Seed

Unconfirmed

1999, VICTORIA, AUSTRALIA

Darren was dumb even for a junkie, but what he lacked in IQ he made up in creativity. In the supermarket, he noticed a bag labeled BIRDSEED 100% POPPY SEED. A hundred percent poppy seed equals a hundred percent opium! Figuring he was onto something good, he seized his chance to circumvent the stranglehold of the international drug cartels. He bought a bag of birdseed, boiled it into a thick black paste, and proceeded to inject the paste into his vein.

Nothing happened, so he did it again.

An hour later he was brought unconscious to the emergency room, as sick as it is possible to be. His chest X-ray showed thousands of tiny seedlike objects scattered throughout his lungfields. The working diagnosis was miliary tuberculosis, so called because the TB deposits resemble millet seeds. Little did the medical team realize the X-ray revealed actual seeds!

Only two weeks later, after he recovered from life-threatening septicemia and multiple organ failure, did the true poppy seed story emerge. Darren survived but subsequently died of a garden-variety overdose.

Reference: Eyewitness account by MedicineMan

Darwin Award: Pining Away

Unconfirmed

Rare Double Darwin!

Three hale and hearty young soldiers had finished their basic training. Before heading out to their respective assignments they decided to spend their few days of leave with one's grandmother, who
lived in the town where they had completed basic training. The
men descended upon Grandmother, who filled them with home cooking and gave them soft beds to sleep in.

Grandmother had a swing job to make **"A case of beer went**
ends meet, so the privates were left alone **into the planning."**
late into the night. They wondered how
they could repay her for her kindness. A
plan began to coalesce from their late-night discussions.

Grandmother had three children. To commemorate the birth of
each child a pine tree had been planted in the front yard. In the fifty
years since the last tree was planted, the pines had grown considerably, and the middle tree now blocked the view from the living-
room window. The privates decided they would cut down that tree,
letting the sun and the view into the room.

A case of beer went into the planning.

To keep the fifty-foot tree from crushing the house the privates
reasoned that they would tie a rope to the top of the tree and pull
the rope away from the house as the tree was cut.

The middle pine, the doomed one, was slightly closer to the house than the others. Two privates climbed an end tree, wound a rope through its upper branches, and threw the rope to a private in the middle tree. He tied the rope around the trunk. By this device they could pull the rope from the ground. The middle pine tree would fall away from the house, and the privates were also clear of the path of the falling tree.

Climbing a pine tree is very sappy work, and scrapes and gouges are inflicted by the natural roughness of its bark. But the hale and hearty privates completed the preliminaries without complaint. The middle tree was lassoed and levered by the rope running through the end tree.

So far, so good.

Two privates were situated on the ground, each straining to pull the tree away from Grandmother's house. The third private revved his thirty-horsepower chainsaw and started to cut. Lo and behold, the tree actually fell away from Grandmother's house! However . . .

The rope-pulling privates had wrapped the rope around their waists, not considering that the falling pine weighed several tons. As the middle pine tree fell, both privates were ripped off their feet and smashed through the branches of the end pine tree. At the height of their acceleration they broke through the top branches of the tree and were briefly airborne before being jerked toward the earth when the middle tree hit the ground. The privates entered into Darwin history, either on the way up through the branches or on the way down to the ground.

The event spoke for itself.

Reference: Eyewitness account of the attending physician

Reader Comments:

"Can't see the forest . . ."

"Sometimes the bark is worse than a bite."

"This is what happens when soldiers don't have officer supervision."

Darwin Award: Into the Abyss

Unconfirmed

An enterprising lumberman had felled a large tree and needed to haul it up a steep embankment. So he jacked up the rear end of his pickup and swapped one of the rear tires for a bare rim. He attached one end of a rope to the rim and the other end of the rope to the felled tree. He put the pickup into gear, expecting the rim to act as a makeshift rope crank that would pull the tree up the embankment, saving him lots of sweat.

"A great idea? Not if you're reading it here!"

A great idea? Not if you're reading it here! You see, the tree vastly outweighed the truck. The man was standing with one foot on the ground and the other foot on the accelerator. When he gunned the engine, the tree acted like an anchor and the truck yanked itself backward. The open door rammed into him, and he was swept over the embankment along with the pickup.

When the dust settled, our lumberman had entered the great beyond. But his escapade served as

Readers point out that unless the truck had a differential lock, this could not happen. The differential gearing on the rear axle would spin the other wheel but not the one with the load. It's the same when you put one rear wheel in a ditch. If that wheel has no grip, power does not go to the wheel still on the road. Agricultural and off-road vehicles often have differential lock, but there is no mention here.

Join the Debate!
www.DarwinAwards.com/book/differential.html

a warning to the next lumberman, who cut up the tree where it lay and carried it off.

Reference: Another brilliant submission from the files of a thirty-year veteran of the ER, who says, "You cannot make this up!"

"If all else fails, Immortality can always be assured by spectacular error."

—John Kenneth Galbraith

Darwin Award: Big Bang Theory

Unconfirmed

OCTOBER 2006, OKLAHOMA

A patient at the local clinic sustained serious internal injuries from a *fishing accident,* including a ruptured eyeball and total hearing loss in one ear. Both legs were amputated midthigh. How did the normally mild sport of fishing become so dangerous?

The man had been standing at the end of a dock with a bucket of dynamite, two-inch chunks, each fused and capped. He took a chunk, lit the fuse, cocked his arm for the throw . . . and dropped the chunk into the bucket of dynamite!

Instantly recognizing the serious situation he was in, the man dove off the dock. But water is incompressible. It transferred the force of the explosion, in line with the blast, against his body.

Besides his other injuries the force also damaged both gonads. One doctor was heard to remark that the gene pool was safe, as this patient had lost his balls.

Reference: Eyewitness account by Mike Andrews

At Risk Survivor: Hedge Your Bets

Unconfirmed

2007, ONTARIO, CANADA

Recently a patient was rushed into the hospital, needing a surgeon to reattach the tips of his fingers to his left hand. While taking the patient history it was found that this bright chap had got the idea of holding his lawn mower sideways and applying it to his hedge. He was holding the mower deck trimming the hedge, and things were going well until the weight of the mower got to be a bit much. He readjusted his grip on the mower deck—and that was when the blade bit him.

> **"He saw his neighbor trimming his hedge with the mower and thought it was a bright idea."**

When the reconstructive plastic surgeon was almost finished with the complex job of sewing the patient back together, another patient came in with the same injury! On questioning him it was found that he, too, had been using his mower to trim his hedge. Apparently he lived near the first patient. He saw his neighbor trimming his hedge with the mower and thought it was a bright idea.

Often fact is so much weirder than fiction.

Reference: Personal account by Northern Scout, whose friend is a plastic surgeon with expertise in reconstructive surgery

Darwin Award:
A Highly Improbable Trajectory
Unconfirmed

A rare nonfatal Darwin Award. Nobody dies!

In a suburban ER the first patient of the evening was a young man suffering from a gunshot wound. His story? "I was at a party and went outside to take a piss. Somebody did a drive-by and shot me." He was examined and a small-caliber entry wound was found at the anterior base of his penis, exiting the midshaft, in and out the right testicle, and into the right thigh where the bullet lodged.

A highly improbable trajectory for a drive-by.

The nurse picked up his white jeans, which had been cut off and thrown aside. Inside the waistband were unmistakable powder burns. She said to him, "You had a gun down your pants!"

At first "Billy the Kid" denied it, but he finally admitted to shooting himself while playing quick-draw with a friend. The reason for the attempted deception? He was on parole for a weapons violation.

The nature of the injury effectively removed him from the gene pool.

Reference: Anonymous eyewitness account

At Risk Survivor:
Tales from the Finnish Forest

Unconfirmed

JULY 2004, FINLAND

I accepted a post as general practitioner for a small village in the Finnish forests. In Scandinavia, Finland is the butt of jokes concerning mosquitoes, trees, and excessive alcohol consumption, so I can't say I hadn't been warned. In defense of the patients, their government had just halved the taxes on alcohol, but nothing could have prepared me for the stories behind the wounds I treated.

CASE 1: A young male I'll call Pekka came in on a Wednesday, as the damages from a weekend of heavy partying began to bother him. Lacerations and abrasions covered his entire backside, from his ankles to the top of his head. But Pekka's main concern was a dislocated thumb. It was sticking out at a ninety-degree angle from his palm and colored a nice shade of purple. I ordered X-rays. Luckily for Pekka he had no fractures, and we reset his thumb joint.

How had these wounds occurred?

Pekka's friend was driving him home from the local waterhole. As they sped along somewhat faster than the speed limit, as one does when one lives in the middle of nowhere, Pekka realized that the driver was as drunk as he was! He decided to take action and get out of the car. While the driver was preoccupied with a sharp bend in the road, Pekka opened the passenger door and quit the car.

Pekka was a regular customer over the summer, coming in when the anesthetic effects of a weekend's libations began to wear off. He had his cast replaced, and the thumb reset, and reset, and reset yet again. I am sure he's still out there working toward a Darwin Award!

CASE 2: A middle-aged woman came in, complaining of a horrible headache. Two days earlier she had been driving to work when she suffered a "blackout" and woke up upside down. Her car was now resting on its roof. She extricated herself and walked (!) to work. But the headache had grown steadily worse. She thought it might be whiplash.

To demonstrate that the pain was worse when she moved her head, she suddenly started shaking her head vigorously back and forth. The nurse and I both jumped to intervene and immobilize her until we could fit a collar and have the madwoman transported by gurney to radiology. She had a fractured cervical vertebra, which luckily had not been displaced even though she'd done her very best right there in my office! She, too, lived to tell the tale.

Reference: Anonymous eyewitness account

Personal Account: Missionary Kid

Unconfirmed

INDONESIA

Darwin says: I have become very fond of these lived-to-tell-the-tale narratives. Many people have survived a brush with death, and their stories make vivid cautionary tales for the younger readers.

I was a missionary kid, nine years old and fascinated with fireworks. My favorite was the Roman candle. You hold one end of a cardboard tube in your hand while the other end shoots pretty colored balls into the air. Then I had a "bright" idea. Wouldn't it be cool to see that stuff shoot out the end of a Coke bottle?

I was nine years old. No sooner said than done! **"Then I had** I pulled out my pocketknife, split some Roman can- **a bright idea."** dles in half, and poured their phosphorous goodness into a Coke bottle. Then, with naive confidence, I lit the match. I still have nightmares about that match at the mouth of the Coke bottle, and I'm forty-one now!

Witnesses said it was the loudest explosion they'd ever heard. The explosion burned off my eyebrows, singed my hair, and peppered me with glass shrapnel. I couldn't hear anything, but apparently I was screaming hysterically and hopping on my one good foot until I collapsed and was carried to the hospital. I spent several hours in surgery, having glass picked out of my body and the tendons above my ankle reattached. They had been severed completely in two.

The top of the Coke bottle was found in the street, fifty feet away. To this day an occasional piece of glass surfaces through my skin! Among my missionary kid friends I am a legend in stupidity for that brilliant event.

Reference: Personal account by Chris Harper, M.D.

"He who hesitates . . . is sometimes saved."

—James Thurber

SCIENCE INTERLUDE: LIFESTYLES
OF THE SLIMY AND CONTAGIOUS
By Steven "DarkSyde" Andrew

Internet surfers and tabloid readers are fascinated by the rich and famous. This tale concerns a young biochemist fascinated with the slimy and contagious! Dr. Herbert Boyer was investigating a common bacteria identified in 1885 by pediatrician Theodor Escherich, who was studying the tragically high rate of infant mortality due to diarrhea when he isolated a rod-shaped microbe in a residue we need not dwell on. The bacteria he discovered now bear his name: *Escherichia coli*, or *E. coli* for short.

You may recognize *E. coli* from the news. Hardly a month goes by without a health advisory issued by the CDC about a new outbreak. Beef, spinach, lettuce—any number of innocuous foods sitting in the crisper of your refrigerator may harbor the killer. There are hundreds of strains of *E. coli*. Most are harmless. But some strains produce potent poisons with the power to cripple their host and bring on the kind of misery that any dehydrated tourist bent over a Mexican toilet can understand. And a few strains are so deadly they could be classified as biological weapons! Still, there's a kinder side to this ubiquitous microbe, a gentler side, a side that serves humanity. Odds are good that one day the humble *E. coli* will serve you too.

After their discovery in 1885 *E. coli* were found in the small intestines of virtually every warm-blooded animal. Several pounds of the bacteria reside in the gastrointestinal tracts of large animals like horses, German shepherds, and, yes, people too. Most strains cause no harm. But researchers came to realize that some strains of the bacteria rampage through the unfortunate host, causing symptoms ranging from lingering malaise to rapid death.

Scientific interest intensified.

Because *E. coli* are widespread and easy to keep alive in the lab, they soon became the most studied microbe in the world. Libraries were filled with sketches and chemical equations describing them. Our understanding of the molecular intricacy of these one-celled creatures grew rapidly. *E. coli* was not a primitive life-form from a forgotten slimy crevice. The bacterium was an exquisitely evolved

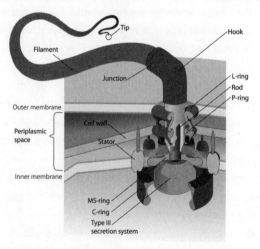

animal, every bit as flexible and cleverly constructed as are we giants of muscle and bone.

They taste the world around them, run the data through a molecular supercomputer, and reconfigure their metabolism to use those nutrients that happen to be available. They build sophisticated defenses against almost any deadly substance that wanders into their domain. When necessary, most can build a flagellum—a tiny motorized propeller that rotates thousands of times a second—and zoom around like high-tech submarines. When food and water are scarce, *E. coli* can even go into stasis (suspended animation)— for years, if necessary.

These transformations are beyond any metamorphosis possible for plants or animals. But *E. coli* reproduce in a matter of hours, so they have had far more relative time, at least as measured by individual generations, to evolve than multicellular plants and animals. To put the talents of *E. coli* into perspective, imagine a herd of horses starving in a drought. If horses were as mutable as *E. coli*, one would morph into a Bengal tiger and eat the rest, and when that food was exhausted, it would sprout wings and fly away. If necessary, it would burrow into the earth and hibernate until rains brought the meadows back. Then it would become a horse again, happily munching on green grass.

When scientists began to sequence DNA, the very code of life, *E. coli* was among the first to be scrutinized. That's when another surprising microbial ability was noticed. *E. coli* were exchanging genes! That wasn't supposed to happen. *E. coli* reproduce by splitting in two, and the daughter cells are identical to the parents. Sex in single-celled organisms? Unthinkable!

Dr. Herbert Boyer was studying the exciting details of gene

exchange when he had a revolutionary idea: If genes from one *E. coli* could be transplanted into another ... could the genes *of a different species* be transplanted into the bacterium? To insert foreign genes Boyer enlisted the help of a plasmid.

A plasmid is a small ring of DNA that carries useful genes. Plasmids are the means by which bacteria swap genes. The realization that bacterial genes are kept not only in the chromosomal DNA, but also on small, transferable rings of DNA, was revolutionary. Plasmids behave very much like the remnant of an independent microbe that struck up a partnership with the ancestral *E. coli*. In return for food and shelter plasmids offer their host a library of useful genes.

The plasmid has an unusual ability. It can acquire random genes from a passing virus, or from the chromosomal DNA of bacteria, and make these genes available to other bacteria. When a bacterium must radically reconfigure itself to survive changing conditions, adaptive genes are often stored on the plasmid. A familiar example is antibiotic drug resistance, which is caused by a protein that inactivates the antibiotic. The gene for the protein, located on a plasmid, is easily transferred between bacteria. Plasmids give *E. coli* the flexibility to quickly adapt to changing conditions.

E. coli has evolved to evolve, via the plasmid.

Boyer realized that he didn't have to insert a gene into the chromosome of the *E. coli*, a tricky maneuver with a low success rate. Instead, the plasmid would do the work for him. Boyer merely had to isolate a plasmid, coax it into accepting a gene of his choosing, then put it back into the *E. coli*. Plasmids are adept at moving useful genes from one *E. coli* to another, and this ability was exactly what Boyer wanted. Once inside, the plasmid should theoretically produce the protein coded by his foreign gene.

Sounds easy? It took thousands of lab hours and years of work before Herbert Boyer's first gene-engineered *E. coli* was confirmed to be a success. By the late 1970s Boyer had created mutants! He knew how to insert genes from wholly different creatures, with a variety of functions, into *E. coli*. If the foreign gene coded for a protein, the bacteria would churn out the substance, while the plasmid was powered, propagated, and protected by the microbe.

Dazzled by the commercial possibilities, Boyer and business friend Robert Swanson invested five hundred dollars each to create a fledgling company and patent this process. And for his invention to be lucrative Boyer decided to program his next designer bacteria to produce a substance with a high demand. A chemical that people wanted and, better yet, needed. He quickly settled on his target: insulin.

Insulin is a small peptide hormone composed of fifty-one amino acids. At the time diabetics were given insulin purified from large mammals such as horses and pigs. It controlled blood sugar levels, but not as effectively as human insulin. Complications from diabetes in general and animal insulin in particular could lead to devastating tissue damage, ruining eyes, heart, liver, or extremities. Animal-derived insulin could trigger rare but life-threatening allergic reactions, yet the only source of human insulin was minuscule (and expensive) amounts obtained from living humans or human cadavers. If Boyer could coerce *E. coli* into making the genuine human version, the mutant bacteria could be grown by the billions in large fermenter vats. Doses of pure human insulin would be unlimited!

And it worked. Humulin is now used by millions of diabetics worldwide. Because it is an exact replica of human insulin, it adds years of life while avoiding the serious side effects of nonhuman insulin. For diabetics who could not tolerate insulin from animal sources, it was the stuff of life itself.

Boyer and other researchers have since created mutant *E. coli* that churn out many useful proteins: human growth hormones to treat dwarfism, blood thinners for heart patients, and an array of other substances. Custom-engineered plasmids themselves have become a robust and lucrative subspecialty in the booming designer microbe industry. The microscopic bacteria have become a laboratory workforce, efficiently and reliably making lifesaving drugs and proteins used for medical research.

For his pioneering contributions to genetic engineering and medicine Herbert Boyer has received academic distinctions. He was awarded the National Medal of Science in 1990. The Yale School of Medicine named its Boyer Center for Molecular Medicine after him. He shared in the prestigious Lemelson–MIT Prize in recognition of his invention. Dr. Herbert Boyer's advances may one day lead to a Nobel Prize.

Oh, and don't forget the small company Boyer and Swanson started with a thousand dollars. They called it Genetic Engineering Technology, or Genentech for short. The two-man firm had been struggling on the edge of bankruptcy, but the promise of Humulin changed all that. In 1980 Genentech went public, using the ticker symbol DNA on the NYSE. The thousand dollars became $130 million overnight, and their shares are worth billions today. Amgen, Biogen, Genzyme, and ImClone rode on the coattails of Genentech's success. Gene-swapping techniques created an entirely new industry, biotechnology, which now employs thousands of highly trained scientists.

Herbert Boyer started out looking into the slimy and contagious, but because of the wealth and recognition he earned, Dr. Boyer's presence would not be amiss on *Lifestyles of the Rich and Famous*!

Steven "DarkSyde" Andrew is a freelance science writer and contributing editor to the popular progressive weblog Daily Kos. He lives in Florida near the Kennedy Space Center with his wife, Mrs. "DS," a dog named Darwin, and a cat named Kali.

CHAPTER 5

CRIMINAL CAPERS

Criminals disregard the laws of men and the laws of physics at their own peril. Scrap metal, munitions, arson, and robbery . . . enjoy the miscellaneous methods that miscreants have devised to bedevil themselves.

Darwin Award: Support Group

Confirmed True by Darwin

28 JULY 2007, CZECH REPUBLIC

Gravity still works.

A pack of thieves attempted to steal scrap metal from an abandoned factory in Kladno. Unfortunately for them, they selected the steel girders that supported the factory roof. When the roof supports were dismantled the roof fell, fatally crushing two thieves and injuring three more.

21 JUNE 2007, PHILIPPINES

Three entrepreneurs planned to profit from stolen scrap metal. They entered a former U.S. military complex and approached the prize: an abandoned water tank. Bedazzled by the potential upside, the three threw logic to the wind and began to cut the metal legs out from under the tank. Guess where it fell? Straight onto the thieves. Their flattened bodies have not yet been identified.

> **"They failed to realize the essential role played by the aptly named 'support.'"**

31 JULY 1997

Two teens were disassembling an electric tower with wrenches when it toppled to the ground. They apparently wanted to sell its aluminum supports for scrap, but they failed to realize the essential role the aptly named "support" plays in a 160-foot tower. One of the men was crushed by the collapse of the ten-thousand-pound tower, while the other dug himself out from under, a sadder but wiser man.

Darwin notes: These thieves are playing a deadly game of Jenga! A new target is the lead roofing of ancient churches. This entire category may soon become too common to win further Awards. See also Barn Razing (page 159).

Reference: Associated Press, CT24 News,
aktualne.centrum.cz, Reuters, GMA-7 News TV, DZEC Radio

Darwin Award: Ammo Dumps

Unconfirmed

2003, IRAQ

When my unit took over an Iraqi ammunition holding area, securing this large piece of real estate was a bit of a problem. Looters periodically showed up to steal brass from the tank and artillery rounds stored in the bunkers. These guys had simple tools: hammers and chisels. And, as ninety-eight percent of Iraqis smoke, this made for an even more interesting day.

One day we saw five looters sneak into a bunker. As we made our way toward the bunker to apprehend them, the bunker exploded. It was a few days before we could get close to the demolished bunker. When we were able to investigate, we ascertained that the looters had either struck a spark while hitting a tank round with hammer and chisel, or one or all were enjoying their finest tobacco while striking the explosive. Either way, the outcome was the demise of five insurgents.

"As we approached to apprehend them, the bunker exploded."

Reference: Anonymous eyewitness account

Reader Comment:

"Do I detect a special spark between us?"

"Only two things are infinite, the universe and human stupidity, and I'm not so sure about the former."

—Albert Einstein

Darwin Award: Thou Shalt Not Steel

Confirmed True by Darwin

8 MARCH 2008, CZECH REPUBLIC

Steel is valuable, especially the high-grade alloy used in steel cable. Scrap metal dealers do not ask questions. They pay in cash. And a good supply of steel cable can be found in elevator shafts.

This particular gold mine was a towering shaft inside an empty granary near Žatec, forty miles northwest of Prague. The cable was tightly fastened, and the far end of it disappeared into the shadowy distance above.

> **"The counterbalance started to move silently downward."**

After substantial wear and tear on a hacksaw, our man finally cut through the strong steel cable. At that instant the counterbalance, no longer held in check, started to move silently downward, accelerating until it reached the bottom of the shaft.

Result: one proud winner of a "terminal velocity" Darwin Award.

R.I.P.

Reference: zpravy.idnes.cz

Reader Comments:

"Shafted!"
"A weighty subject."

Darwin Award: A Slow Burn

Confirmed True by Darwin

6 JULY 2006, OHIO

A rare Double Darwin!

Insurance fraud is harder than it looks. Just ask Musa and his son Essa, who hired an arsonist to burn down their Steak Thyme sub shop so they could collect the insurance money. They promised the arsonist a sixty-thousand-dollar-a-year job, although where he would work once the shop was ashes is unknown.

Three times he tried and three times he failed to destroy the sandwich shop. Whether it was a Molotov cocktail thrown through the window, or chairs doused with gasoline and set ablaze, the result was the same. Minor damage. The neighborhood was up in arms over the apparent "hate crimes" repeatedly being committed against the two Jordanian immigrants.

Musa grew tired of throwing good money after bad. This was getting him nowhere! For the fourth arson attempt, only twelve hours after the flaming chairs fizzled, he and his son decided to help the hired hand. They spread gasoline liberally around their eatery. A single match would do the trick.

After the third bungled arson Musa boasted in a televised interview, "If someone is trying to shut me out of business, it's not going to happen. This is my life and nobody's going to take that away from me." Nobody but himself!

"Three times he tried, and three times he failed."

Tragically, they had more talent for arson than their amateur arsonist. They took a cigarette break and one flick of a lighter later, a gas explosion took out one wall and burned both men so severely that, despite several weeks of hospitalized care, the men died.

Reference: WCPO News, Associated Press, Coalition Against Insurance Fraud

Reader Comments:

"If you want something done right . . ."
"It would have been easier to just run their business. . . ."

Darwin Award: Crutch, Meet Crotch

Confirmed True by Darwin

NOVEMBER 2007, RUSSIA

Late one night Eduard entered the apartment of a thirty-year-old handicapped man, who slept peacefully as Eduard quietly cleaned out the valuables. Eduard was preparing to leave when suddenly the man woke up.

"I couldn't believe my eyes! The dark shape of some goon was standing next to my nightstand!" recalled the burglary victim. "I cried out and he attacked me, who was defenseless, with his fists! I had no choice. I hit him between the legs with my crutch and he leapt out the window. Thank God I live on the first floor, and he did not die from the fall.

"I did not understand at first what had fallen out of his pants. When I looked closer, I realized that it was a testicle, a man's testicle! I put it in cold water and rushed to the phone." The handicapped man dialed emergency services several times, but "the doctors hung up on me when I told them I had ripped a burglar's balls off!"

> **"I had no choice. I hit him between the legs with my crutch."**

Half an hour later the blood-covered thief was found lying on the sidewalk by a passerby, who called the police. When the medics revived the unconscious man, he started screaming hysterically, "Give me back my balls!"

Eduard's genitals were so traumatized that doctors had to amputate the entire scrotum to prevent gangrene. In the hospital the burglar filed a complaint against his victim. He said, "I will never forgive him!"

Reference: cripo.com.ua

Reader Comments:

"That'll fix him."
"Crotchety old man."
"Something is missing. . . ."
"In a high-pitched voice: 'OH, MY GOD!' "

Darwin Award: Descent of Man

Unconfirmed

NEW YORK

In twenty years on the NYPD I witnessed plenty of ill-considered death and mayhem. In one case we responded to a body-in-a-courtyard call. We found a nineteen-year-old man who had obviously perished by falling from a great height. We ruled out suicide, as access to the roof was secure, and there were no open windows. Eventually we located an informative eyewitness.

The man's younger brother told us that the two of them had intended to burglarize an apartment. His brother had climbed a cable TV wire to a fifth-floor window and, while struggling to force the window, had lost his grip on the thin cable and fallen to his death. The brother panicked and ran.

When I asked why they had selected that particular apartment, the brother looked at me incredulously and replied, "Obviously they got a TV if they got a cable going in the window."

Reference: Eyewitness account by an NYPD police officer

Darwin Award: On the Piste

Confirmed True by Darwin

2 FEBRUARY 2008, ITALY

David, forty-six, was sliding down an Italian ski slope one night, riding on padding that he had removed from the safety barriers at the bottom of the run. It did not occur to him that it might be dangerous to sled down the same slope from which he had stolen protective padding.

Sauze d'Oulx is one of five villages that make up the Milky Way ski area in northern Italy. Popular with British skiers, the resort is known for its party atmosphere. A ski resort spokesperson for Sauze d'Oulx said, "The men had all been drinking when they tore off the padding, and ironically . . ."

. . . they careened straight into the bare barriers at the bottom of the piste (groomed slope). David died from head and chest injuries inflicted by the unpadded metal. Two of

"The ski area is known for its party atmosphere."

his friends survived with medical attention. Another Darwin Award candidate is still missing after he wandered away "bloodied and distressed."

Reference: UK *Daily Telegraph*, dailymail.co.uk

Darwin Award: Slippery When Wet

Confirmed True by Darwin

15 JANUARY 2008, SWEDEN

The Darwin Awards have celebrated many boneheaded things bur-glars do in the commission of their crimes. For instance, taking a shortcut down a fifty-five-foot sheer rock face.

Early one morning two men broke into a gymnasium (high school) east of Stockholm. After a profitable stroll through the school, they were startled by a janitor. They raced out of the build-ing into the predawn darkness. Fearing imminent detection, they took a shortcut to safety—down the face of a steep fifty-five-foot rock escarpment. But in selecting this convenient shortcut they failed to consider three crucial facts:

First, it was pitch-black. Due to the northern latitude the sun rises late in Sweden.

Second, it had rained during the night.

"This is the province of mountain goats, not humans hoping to pass on their genes."

And third, the rock in eastern Sweden is granite, the type of rock that is pol-ished into posh floors and fancy counter-tops. The danger of slippery granite is a well-known fact for residents of the area.

Escaping down a granite cliff, in the rain, in the dark? Try tilting a slab of polished granite, pouring water over it, and making a controlled descent while carrying a load of loot. This is the province of mountain goats, not humans hoping to pass on their genes. In short, one of the burglars slipped and fell head over heels to his death, bringing a new meaning to *the crack of dawn.*

He was found with his worldly riches scattered around him.

Reference: aftonbladet.se

"The best laid schemes of mice and men go oft astray."

—Robert Burns

Darwin Award: Four Great Ideas

Unconfirmed

25 MARCH 2007, OREGON

Anthony was stopped for speeding. The vehicle that the twenty-year-old was driving checked out as stolen in Idaho. The deputy called for backup and placed the suspect and his passengers in separate patrol cars. Here, Anthony had his first great idea! He thought he could outsmart the police, a notion that often proves harmful to the perp.

"He thought he could outsmart the police, a notion that often proves harmful." While the officers had their backs turned, Anthony managed to move his handcuffed hands from behind to in front of his body. His second great idea was to wiggle through the small window to the front seat of the patrol car. His third great idea? He drove off in the patrol car, never mind the state patrol officers and deputies from two counties.

Naturally, Anthony wished to elude pursuit. He did so by driving ninety miles an hour, passing some cars and forcing others off the road. He was rapidly approaching the city of Lakeview when he encountered spike strips placed in his way by the police. But not even the setback of flat tires slowed him down. He thought he could still control the disabled car and outrun the police!

We will never know what he might have done if he had reached Lakeview. Following standard procedure, a state patrolman rammed the rear quarter panel of the stolen police cruiser, a move designed to spin and slow the car. But due to the flat tire and Anthony's erratic driving the vehicle spun off the road and rolled.

Anthony's final mistake? He had neglected to fasten his seat belt. He was thrown from the car and died a week later. Whether or not he managed to learn anything during that final week of reflection, one hopes that others will.

Reference: Anonymous eyewitness account

"Life is wasted on the living."

—Douglas Adams

At Risk Survivor: Red-Hot Chili Peppers
Unconfirmed

One day an inmate stole a bag of jalapeño peppers in juice. Kitchen work is coveted by inmates because of these fringe benefits. He stuffed the plastic bag down the front of his pants. But as he attempted his getaway, the bag burst. In an attempt to cool the fires the prisoner jumped into the shower. It was winter and there was only one water temperature: hot. This only made matters worse!

The inmate was subsequently nicknamed "Crispy Balls."

Reference: Eyewitness account by Karmyn Crabb

Reader Comment:

"Goodness Gracious, Great Balls of Fire!"

SCIENCE INTERLUDE:
EVOLUTION IS SCREWY

By Jason Stevens, Darwin Awards philosopher

When children ask about reproduction, the storks-bring-babies story eventually gives way to a discussion of "the birds and the bees." Such talks may be only slightly more enlightening than the stork fable. Much can be said about bee reproduction without revealing insights into the human process. Avian biology is more diverse but also provides an awkward platform from which to launch a discussion about human sexuality.

Most birds have nothing much resembling human sex organs. Most male and female birds possess internal reproductive systems leading to a single, multipurpose opening known as the cloaca. Virtuoso courtship songs, dazzling visual displays, and even sophisticated nest constructions play roles in the selection of mates. Yet the genetic transfer itself typically involves no more contact than an act poetically characterized as the "cloacal kiss."

However, ornithologists have long known that some bird species do have a male phallus and a female vagina. In dramatic cases this is impossible to overlook. To wit, the Argentine lake duck sports a male member that may exceed the length of the animal's own body. Though that is an extreme example, many other species of duck are endowed with relatively long penises ... often in the shape of a corkscrew!

Previous generations of scientists did not investigate the subject in great depth. Nature provides a vast array of spectacular subjects to study without venturing into territory one's peers may regard as lascivious. Yet by 2001, when *Nature* published a brief report raising questions about links between duck penis traits and reproductive selection, the time had come for curiosity to vanquish reluctance.

Enter Dr. Patricia Brennan. Initially her interest in ducks stemmed from a specific academic inquiry. Various species exhibit different frequencies of behavior clinically described as "forced copulation." Since all these modern species evolved from a common ancestor species, ducks are ideal subjects for investigating the influence of forced copulation on physical evolution.

"When I saw my first [duck] phallus, I cannot even describe to you what I felt. It's the most amazing organ that you will ever see," Dr. Brennan recollects. Not only are some duck penises long, and not only are some spiral-shaped, but some are even equipped with a feathery tip! To understand the basis for all this anatomical variation Dr. Brennan decided to examine reproductive systems in female ducks.

The results would surprise almost anyone but a duck. Females did not simply have a vaginal canal long enough to accommodate the phallus of a compatible drake. In species featuring a coil in the male phallus, vaginas spiral in the opposite direction. This intensifies the degree of struggle required to accomplish fertilization without cooperation. Some females also developed branching canals, complete with musculature to divert a penis from the proper canal to an infertile sac. Without a relaxed and compliant mate, these features dramatically reduce a male's chances of successful fertilization.

The emerging picture suggested that duck reproduction was as far removed from the avian cloacal kiss as the cheetah's sprint is from the ponderous stride of the sloth. Yet crucial questions remained. Were the unusual features of ducks' phalluses similar to the male peacock's train, adapted to an extreme because presentation plays a crucial role in sexual selection? Or was this instead a sort of evolutionary battle with each side escalating to gain control over the fertilization process?

> The feathery tip of a male duck phallus, a feature of those species most extreme in their incidence of forced copulation, appears to be used to swab out seminal fluid deposited by a prior mating. Observational data indicates that females also discourage fertilization through behaviors such as using water to cleanse themselves internally after an unwanted mating.

Bird mating behaviors have long drawn the attention of ornithologists and hobbyist birdwatchers alike. Consider some of the spectacular techniques males employ to gain the attention of receptive females.

- Zebra finch *(Taeniopygia guttata)*—elaborate and loud birdsong
- Greater bird of paradise *(Paradisaea apoda)*—competitive dancing displays
- Northern cardinal *(Cardinalis cardinalis)*—eye-catching red coloration

- Great frigate bird *(Fregata minor)*—large inflatable throat bladder
- Satin bowerbird *(Ptilonorhynchus violaceus)*—ornately decorated love nests

Based on the mating behavior of other bird species the case for a long male duck phallus as a visual enticement had some merit. Yet this did not explain why the reproductive anatomy of female ducks seemed adapted as much to frustrate as to accommodate the exotic endowments of their counterparts. Dr. Brennan advanced the hypothesis that the real driving force behind these adaptations was "postcopulatory competition." To gather data she and her collaborators scrutinized the behavior and anatomy of sixteen species of waterfowl.

A complex empirical process known as phylogenetic analysis was able to establish that the unusual shapes in male and female duck genitalia evolved in tandem. This view of coevolution is further supported by a simple fact confirming one of Dr. Brennan's key predictions. From one duck species to another the complexity of genital morphology varies in clear correlation with the incidence of forced copulation! This analysis enabled scientists to make precise predictions about the shape of duck features yet to be examined. Testable predictions are an essential part of the scientific process.

All that twisty anatomy is evolution's response to the conflicting goals of males and females. Male ducks seek to produce as many offspring as possible, while female ducks seek the best father for a clutch of eggs. Drakes may attempt fertilization via forced copulation, but hens resist by refusing to relax a complex vaginal canal or by offering up reproductive dead ends to unwelcome mates. The mechanisms male ducks evolved to usurp the prerogative of sexual selection are marginalized by female countermeasures.

The fact that some species of duck feature a long corkscrew penis is an intriguing observation. The complexities of female genitalia in those species are no less intriguing. Solving the puzzle of their interrelationship required research into areas that had previously received little scientific attention. Particular findings in that work added testable new knowledge to human understanding of sexual selection's role in evolution. Researchers have opened a new window into the process by which complex social interactions can result in the evolution of some astonishing physical features.

The responsibility to tell a young person about "the birds and the bees" is a daunting one. Yet it may be possible to take solace from the study of birds. Were we less like humans and more like ducks, explaining reproduction and sexuality to the next generation would be considerably more complicated than it actually is.

Brennan, P. L., R. O. Prum, K. G. McCracken, M. D. Sorenson, R. E. Wilson, et al., 2007. Coevolution of Male and Female Genital Morphology in Waterfowl. *PLoS ONE*. 2(5): e418. plosone.org/doi/pone.0000418.

Catlin, Roger. July 11, 2007. Duck Sex. *TV Eye*. blogs.courant.com/roger_catlin _tv_eye/2007/07/duck-sex.html.

McCracken, Kevin G., Robert E. Wilson, Pamela J. McCracken, Kevin P. Johnson, September 13, 2001. Are ducks impressed by drakes' display? *Nature*. 413: 138.

Williams, Liz. May 3, 2007. Duck genitals locked in arms race. Cosmos Online. www.cosmosmagazine.com/node/1277.

Bowerbird mating techniques: www.msri.org/ext/larryg/pages/15.htm

Scheduled for a Halloween delivery in 1972, **Jason Stevens** wisely postponed his birthdate until November 12. The years to follow would see him learning to walk, talk, and program primitive computers with line-numbered BASIC. His lifelong interest in science and technology is joined by interests in the performing arts, politics, history, and philosophy. During his college years he earned distinction as a member of the Bradley University Speech Team and rent money as a board operator/announcer for public radio's WCBU-FM. Since then he helped establish two short-lived small businesses, played keyboards with an even more short-lived rock band, and typed an unknown number of gratuitously long sentences. The publication of this piece constitutes a milestone in his ongoing quest for prosaic succinctness.

CHAPTER 6

WORK WOES

We spend a large number of our waking hours at work. Due to shortcuts, boredom, and inattention to safety our waking hours are often ended by work accidents. Nuclear plants, boats, farm workers, demolition experts, teachers, and welders give their all for their jobs. The lighter side of work!

Darwin Award: Absolutely Radiant

Confirmed True by Darwin

10 DECEMBER 1968, OZYORSK, RUSSIA

While researching nuclear accidents a physicist found this Darwin Award. The following report is quoted directly from a Los Alamos review document, with a few sentences added to help make the situation clear to the layperson.

Mayak is a nuclear fuel processing center in central Russia that was experimenting with plutonium purification techniques. The report states that they were using "an unfavorable geometry vessel in an improvised operation as a temporary vessel for storing plutonium organic solution." In other words they were pouring liquid plutonium into an unsafe container.

Keep an eye on the shift supervisor.

"It was noticed that the solution was a combination of organic and aqueous solution [gunk in the tank]. Two operators [instructed by the shift supervisor] used an improvised setup to decant the dark brown [concentrated plutonium] organic solution. The shift supervisor then left to tend to other duties. During the second filling of the bottle a mixture of aqueous *and* organic solution was drawn in. As a result the operators stopped filling the bottle."

One asked the shift supervisor for further instructions. He was told to continue decanting the solution. This operator "poured it into the sixty-liter vessel for a second time. After [most] of the solution had been poured out, the operator saw a flash of light and felt a pulse of heat. Startled, the operator dropped the bottle, ran down the stairs, and from the room."

The plutonium was too concentrated, and he had accidentally started a nuclear chain reaction! The alarms sounded, and everyone evacuated. So far, no fatal errors. But a second criticality happened while everyone was safely underground. Here's where it gets good.

"The shift supervisor insisted that the radiation control supervisor permit him to enter the work area. The radiation control supervisor resisted but finally accompanied the shift supervisor back into the building. As they approached the basement room where the accident had occurred, the radiation levels continued to rise. The radiation control supervisor prohibited the shift supervisor from proceeding. In spite of the prohibition the shift supervisor deceived the radiation control supervisor and entered the room."

"He deceived the radiation control supervisor and entered the room. . . ."

So, with things more or less under control, the shift supervisor tricks the radiation control supervisor and goes into the room full of plutonium.

His "subsequent actions were not observed by anyone. However, there was evidence that he attempted to pour [the plutonium] into a floor drain. His actions caused a third excursion, larger than the first two, activating the alarm system in both buildings."

The shift supervisor had proceeded to set off an even bigger nuclear chain reaction!

"The shift supervisor, covered in plutonium organic solution, immediately returned to the underground tunnel. He died about one month after the accident," having received four times the fatal dose of radiation. Everyone else survived.

Even if the shift supervisor had lived, he would still qualify for a Darwin Award. That much radiation causes sterility!

Reference: "A Review of Criticality Accidents," 2000 revision, Los Alamos National Laboratory document LA-13638; elucidated by Edmund Schluessel

Reader Comments:

"A flash of insight."
"Now hiring: Nuclear Plant Shift Supervisor."

Darwin Award: Pierced!

Confirmed True by Darwin

JANUARY 2008, PENNSYLVANIA

A twenty-three-year-old man with various body piercings decided to have some fun at work. He wondered, "What would it feel like to connect the electronic control tester to my chest piercings?" Several coworkers tried to convince him that it was a bad idea to wire himself up to the electronic device, but he ignored their pleas.

"What would it feel like to . . ."

He proceeded to connect two alligator clips to his metal nipple piercings, one on each side, and hit the test button. . . .

His coworkers were still trying to revive him with CPR and rescue breathing when the police and rescue personnel arrived. They were not successful.

Reference: *The Boyertown Area Times,* PA. January 10, 2008.
Vol. 150, Number 32. berksmontnews.com

Reader Comments:

"I would not even try this with my pierced earrings."
"Shock to the heart, and you're to blame. . . ."—Bon Jovi
"All charged up."

Darwin Award: Barn Razing

Unconfirmed

14 JANUARY 2007, WEST VIRGINIA

Raising a new barn is an endeavor that brings a community together. Demolishing a barn is another question. A trio of friends set
out to dismantle a dilapidated structure one bracing winter afternoon. Speaking of bracing . . .

It was all fun and games until one industrious fellow fired up his
chainsaw and ripped through a crucial support post. Carrying the
weight of a full barn roof, those wooden beams were all that stood
between the demolition worker and structural collapse.

The roof succumbed to the pull of gravity, and the ill-fated lum-
berjack had only a brief moment to contemplate the approach of his
deadly problem. As a consolation prize, the deceased was indeed
successful at demolishing the barn.

Reference: *Hampshire Review*

Reader Comment:

"Gravity hurts. Gravity + Wood hurts more."

Darwin Award: A Prop-er Send-off

Unconfirmed

BROOME, AUSTRALIA

When you work as a diver on a pearl farm, there are many ways to "buy the farm." Our head diver, Mitchell, known as Sharky, was not afraid to take risks to get the job done. He was a loose gun in a company of cowboys. Sharky seemed destined to make an original exit.

A near miss happened in Roebuck Bay. He miscalculated the amount of fuel needed for the air compressor

"Instead of following standard procedure . . ."

that pumps air to the divers below. Instead of following standard procedure—bringing everyone up and refueling during a surface interval—he surfaced alone to top up the fuel tank while the compressor was still running.

The deck was unsteady, and naturally he spilled some petrol. The compressor had been running for hours. Its red-hot exhaust ignited the spilled fuel, and the flames followed the fuel into the tank. The brand-new dive boat was fully kitted out for the pearl farm, including oxygen for resuscitations. The resulting mushroom cloud explosion from the oxy bottle startled observers all the way back in town, five kilometers away.

Luckily Sharky jumped back in the water before the big explosion. He and his crew were picked up by another dive boat.

Despite this incident Sharky was promoted to skipper of a larger vessel. However, the skipper still found excuses to don the old dive gear. One such excuse was a mooring rope tangled around the propeller. Instead of asking an outfitted diver for assistance, Sharky chucked on his dive gear, started the compressor, clipped on a dive hose, and jumped off the back of the boat. But he neglected to take the boat out of gear. . . .

The spinning prop entangled his hose and started reeling him in. His "lifeline" pulled him through the prop, and he died on the way to the hospital. Sharky didn't have any children (that he knew of), but he did have a wicked sense of humor. He died doing what he always did . . . having a go.

Reference: Eyewitness account by Anonymous, who says,
"I hope he forgives me for submitting him for a Darwin Award!"

Darwin Award: Crushing De'feet

Confirmed True by Darwin

28 NOVEMBER 2006, AUSTRIA

A man who had been reported missing was found the following morning in a trash compactor, victim of an industrial accident. Once the videotape from a monitoring camera was reviewed, all became clear.

He worked for a parcel delivery service in Hall in Tirol. He had loaded the hydraulic press with empty boxes and started it up. At that point the longtime employee walked to the edge of the filling hole and used his foot to press the boxes farther into the hydraulic trash compactor.

> **"He used his foot to press the boxes into the hydraulic compactor."**

His foot was seized by the press, and he was drawn into the chamber and crushed. He was not discovered until his colleagues needed to use the press again the next day.

Reference: tirol.orf.at

Darwin Award:
Chemistry Went to Her Head

Confirmed True by Darwin

2 FEBRUARY 2008, BULGARIA

It was a cold but sunny February afternoon. Anna, a biology teacher from Sofia, was driving two friends home from a memorial service. Suddenly the vehicle stopped. Bystanders saw all three occupants dash from the car to a nearby manhole and start pouring down liquids and powders from various bottles and jars.

Apparently, the biology teacher had been performing chemistry experiments in her free time and had some leftover noxious chemicals. It is still not entirely clear what the chemicals were, but two of the bottles were labeled diethyl ether and methanol, both highly flammable liquids. The former is also used as a sedative, so one explanation for their actions is that they felt dizzy from the ether vapors and thought it was a good idea to pour them in the sewer.

As it turns out, a good idea it definitely was not. The cocktail of flammable substances in the enclosed space of the sewer caused an explosion so powerful that it launched the manhole cover into the air, decapitating the (briefly) surprised Anna. Left without a head on her shoulders, she decided it was time to kick the bucket.

> "Tossing random chemicals down the drain is not as wise as it might first appear."

The other two people were not unharmed, but were alive. They were taken to the hospital with burns on their faces. They may not

regain their eyesight, but hopefully will be able to speak clearly enough to tell their children that tossing random chemicals down the drain is not as wise as it might first appear.

Reference: focus-news.net

"Darwin Award contenders would do well to remember the wise words of Brooke Shields:
'If you're killed, you've lost a very important part of your life.'"

Darwin Award: Silage Spreader

Unconfirmed

1992, UK

I am an injury lawyer, and for many years I represented the National Farmers' Union Mutual, an insurance company specializing in (yep) farms. Farmworkers do the most insane things that never ceased to amaze me, but this one takes the biscuit.

I was investigating a fatal accident on a farm in Hampshire. The deceased, an experienced hand, drove a silage spreader hitched to a tractor. Molasses was added to the spreader by parking it beneath a molasses tank and opening the tap. The silage was mixed by three large steel augers rotating in the belly of the open-topped spreader. The tractor was then driven into the fields, and the feed mix merrily flung far and wide from the spreader.

To access the molasses tap one climbs a ladder fixed to the tank. The subsequent inquest made it clear that our man, finding he had parked a mite short and could not reach **"So he could save himself time . . ."** the tap, decided not to get down and move the tractor five feet but rather to teeter along the edge of the open spreader hopper (a metal rim some three inches wide) wearing wellies covered in the usual farm muck, so he could save himself twenty seconds of precious work time.

Needless to say, time being so dear, he did not bother to disengage the PTO shaft of the tractor, which meant he was doing his balancing act above three bloody great steel augers rotating below him. Pity the poor workmate who eventually wondered why the tractor had been sitting there for an hour chugging gently away, put two and two together, and took a peep into the hopper.

Reference: Eyewitness account by Mike Clarke

Reader Comments:

"Going down on the farm."
"A sticky situation."

"All life is an experiment."

—Ralph Waldo Emerson

Darwin Award: A Breathtaking View

Unconfirmed

1989, SOUTH AFRICA

Downtown Johannesburg is continuously growing with the construction of modern new buildings. One such building was designed with a steel framework, intended to be clad in glass as a final touch.

On the eighteenth floor an engineer was inspecting the framework. He asked one of the workers to stand on a scaffold that was projecting through an open space where the glass panel would soon be mounted. With the worker acting as a counterweight, the engineer walked out onto the scaffold, checked the exterior, and came back in to continue his inspection.

After the engineer left, curiosity got the better of the worker. He walked out on the scaffold to see what the engineer had been looking at.... Fortunately the falling worker did not take out any pedestrians!

The worker removed himself from the gene pool out of sheer stupidity. But one

> **"Curiosity got the better of the worker."**

does wonder whether that engineer is blithely continuing to ask trusting people to act as counterweights without explaining his reason, and leaving a trail of bodies in his wake!

Reference: Eyewitness account of a person
who was on lunch break when she saw the man fall

Reader Comments:

"Curiosity killed the cat!"
"Uhhh what was he looking at?"
"When engineers assume others are thinking the same thing."

Darwin Award: Breathless

Confirmed True by Darwin

2007

An experienced forty-seven-year-old rescue diver was filming an underwater video of a wreck forty-four meters below sea level. He was in deep water, nine meters deeper than the recreational diving maximum, which warrants special training and extra safety considerations. To keep the audio track clear he turned off the alarms on his dive computer. His buddy, working on the other side of the wreck, did the same.

Defeating the safety . . . harbinger of so many Darwin Awards.

Sixteen minutes into the dive he was alone and out of air—a situation that should never sneak up on a diver. But he had turned off the safety alarms and swum out of sight of his buddy. The diver made an emergency ascent up the anchor line. At eighteen meters the divemaster tried to assist him, but the panicked diver refused to take an alternate air source. He continued his rapid flight to the surface, where he lost consciousness and could not be revived.

"The bends" are a painful and occasionally fatal condition caused by nitrogen bubbles surging into the bloodstream and tissues due to a too-rapid ascent, but they can be avoided if a diver follows the dive table limits and makes a decompression stop while ascending to allow blood gas levels to normalize. Air embolism is damage to the lungs due to a diver holding his breath on ascent. The volume of air doubles every ten meters one rises.

The cause of death: "Air embolism due to rapid ascent."

Was it an accident? This experienced diver deliberately disregarded two basic safety rules: Pay attention to your gauges and stay within reach of your buddy. If he had

"The experienced diver deliberately disregarded two basic safety rules."

attended to his gauges (and not turned off the alarms) he could have made a controlled ascent, including a decompression stop for safety. If he was near his buddy, they could have shared air as they both made a controlled ascent. Either precaution would have saved his life.

Reference: *Alert Diver* magazine, "Breathless on the Bottom," March/April 2007

At Risk Survivor: He Kicked the Bucket

Confirmed True by Darwin

26 JANUARY 2007, TEXAS

In a world full of wonders man invented boredom. So work time becomes playtime. If you work in an office, you reproduce your naughty bits on the copy machine. If you work for an arc welding company? A plastic bucket, welding materials, and a single spark can combine for a playdate with a bang.

"I was on the computer when I heard the boom," said a resident of the trailer park adjacent to the welding shop. "It shook my house. The whole neighborhood could feel it!"

Just for kicks a thirty-year-old welder and four coworkers had attempted to blow up a plastic bucket. Our man placed a striker, a spark-generating device used to start a welder's torch, in **"Just for kicks, they attempted to blow up a bucket."** the plastic bucket and sealed it. Then he filled the bucket with acetylene, an explosive gas used for welding. The plan was to toss the bucket in the air and watch it explode when the striker sparked.

Before that happened, however, our Darwin wannabe inadvertently kicked the plastic bucket, and the striker struck a spark. BOOM. The explosive force turned the lid of the bucket into a whirling saw that flew through the air and struck the man in his right arm, nearly severing it. He also sustained lacerations to his right leg.

No one else was injured in the blast, and no charges were filed, as it was felt that the perpetrator of the incident had already been sufficiently punished.

Reference: Galveston County *Daily News*

At Risk Survivor: Flyswatter

Confirmed True by Darwin

APRIL 2004, CALIFORNIA

One spring morning when a bug crawled across his desk, an adult education teacher gave twenty-five students an impromptu and involuntary lesson in safety—during his safety class. You see, Teach had an unusual paperweight, a 40 mm shell he had found on a hunting trip. It made a unique conversation piece. Using opaque reasoning, he assumed that the ordnance *must* be inert. But this particular ordnance was the teacher's ticking ticket to fame.

Back to the spring morning when a bug crawled across his desk. Should he squash it with a tissue? Sweep it out the door? Leave it to pursue its happy existence and continue with his lesson? No, the teacher picked another alternative. He hefted the "inert" artillery shell and slammed it onto the short-lived insect.

> "He assumed the artillery shell *must* be inert."

The impact set off the primer, and the resulting explosion caused burns and shrapnel lacerations on his hand, forearm, and torso. No one else in the classroom was hurt. To the teacher's further consolation his actions did succeed in one respect. That bug was eliminated.

Reference: cnn.com, *San Mateo Daily News*

At Risk Survivor: Caulker Burner

Unconfirmed

SEPTEMBER 1999, SCOTLAND

The Ferguson shipyard at Port Glasgow uses a plasma cutter to cut steel for boats according to plans. For smaller holes the plasma torch just cuts out the hole. But for larger holes it is programmed to leave sections of uncut steel to make sure that no one can accidentally fall through.

Once the steelwork is positioned on the ship, a caulker burner uses an oxyacetylene blowtorch to burn through the six-inch sections, thereby creating the properly sized hole in the steel.

Enter our hero. Liam was a caulker burner, and he had been tasked with the job of going onto the ship and cutting away these sections. The piece in question had been designed to allow a large exhaust pipe to come through the deck.

Liam began his task of burning away the steel. But Liam had decided to stand in the middle of the hole he was burning out, which led to a rather nasty fifteen-foot fall onto scaffolding below. He escaped with a few broken ribs and a month off work. Luckily for him, neither the blowtorch nor the large steel plate fell on top of him, therefore denying him a gloriously well-deserved Darwin Award.

> "He decided to stand in the middle of the hole he was burning out."

Reference: *Greenock Telegraph* and the eyewitness account of E. Buchanan, a twelve-year veteran of the shipyards

At Risk Survivor: The Turn of the Screw
Unconfirmed
WESTERN AUSTRALIA

The Kalgoorlie Nickel Smelter uses a piece of heavy machinery called a screw feeder, a large cast-iron tube with an Archimedean screw inside. As the screw turns, it transports chunks of ore along its length. One of the drawbacks to the design is that it can and does jam, if ore gets wedged between the edge of the screw and the casing.

When a jam occurs, correct procedure is . . . what? That's right, shut down the machinery, open a hatch in the casing, and use a pry bar to dislodge the jam. Then start the machinery back up.

Incorrect procedure, as demonstrated by one worker, is to take a six-foot jimmy bar and bash the side of the casing in an effort to dislodge the jam. This is a bad idea because cast iron can fracture if abused. But the screw feeder is a rugged piece of equipment. It survived the bashing.

Our antihero then opened the inspection panel while the feeder was running. He spotted the jam and dislodged it with the same six-foot jimmy bar. Did I mention that the feeder was still running? Did I mention that it's a large and rugged piece of equipment?

"He put an end to the smelter's accident-free run in a public and highly amusing fashion."

The screw grabbed the end of the jimmy bar and whipped it around violently. The free end of the bar intersected our man's testicles. He landed in a crumpled, semiconscious heap ten feet away from the now free-running feeder. Fortunately for him the mangled bar missed him when it was flung free of the feeder moments later; otherwise this story would have a more somber ending.

The unfortunate worker sustained injuries to his genitalia that necessitated a hospital stay. And worse yet, he put an end to the smelter's accident-free run in a public and highly amusing fashion. His pride was as crushed as his testicles. Almost.

Kalgoorlie is a mining town as famous for its hotels, hookers, and gambling as it is for being the center of Australia's gold fields. But even by Kal's standards this one was a ripper.

Reference: Eyewitness account of Mat Meyer, who says,
"My younger brother worked at the Kalgoorlie Nickel Smelter.
He was laughing so hard telling this story that he nearly wet himself."

Reader Comment:

"Talk about a workplace fling!"

SCIENCE INTERLUDE:
THE GREAT DYING

By Norm Sleep

SIBERIA, FEBRUARY, LATE PERMIAN PERIOD
252 MILLION YEARS AGO

In the Arctic night a herd of dicynodonts (mammal-like ox-sized reptiles) huddled against the polar wind. They nibbled small leaves exposed by the blowing snow in the dim light. Suddenly the ground lurched. The animals had felt numerous earthquakes. They bared their twin tusks and roared, fearfully looking up for rocks that might cascade upon them. But then quiet returned, and the herd went back to its grazing.

However, this was no ordinary quake. The shaking resumed and became more intense. On the horizon to the north a pillar of fire erupted, bringing a false dawn. Then, only a few hundred meters from the herd, the earth cracked open. The crack exploded into a chasm that soon extended to both horizons. Lava poured to the surface, followed by deafening detonations. Red-hot gas spewed from the crack, and glowing coal and rock fragments pelted through the air. A dense hot cloud of gas blew across the Siberian landscape, incinerating the trees in its path.

The dicynodonts fled, but nowhere was safe.

Local vicissitudes such as volcanoes and earthquakes are common over geological time. They remove countless individual organisms from the gene pool but usually have little effect on evolution. This time, however, the effect of the eruption was global and catastrophic. Seventy-five percent of land species and ninety-five percent of marine species would soon be extinct.

Geology of the Eruption

Beneath the grazing dicynodonts a giant pool of lava had welled up from the base of the lithosphere one hundred kilometers down. At forty kilometers the lava reached the earth's crust and accumulated beneath the buoyant and deformable lower crustal rocks. Hours before the dicynodonts' doom a crack opened above the lava pool. A river of lava rushed toward the surface of the planet.

Just before the lava reached the surface, it intruded on a vast coal bed that happened to lie a few hundred meters below the surface. Coal is less dense than lava. The lava took the path of least resistance right through the coal bed, spreading through it far from the initial crack.

The Siberian coals contained pore water and hydrocarbons. When lava hit the coal beds, the hydrocarbons turned to gas, just as happens today in coking plants. The heavier tar hydrocarbons "cracked" into smaller molecules, creating more gas. The red-hot coals reacted with the pore water to form coal gas, composed of methane and carbon monoxide, with smaller amounts of other hydrocarbons. All of these heated gases then started to expand.

In some places the surface of the earth collapsed into the coal bed, releasing gas. Elsewhere, the incandescent gas followed the lava up cracks. When the hydrocarbons, carbon monoxide, and methane came into contact with the oxygen in the air, they ignited, causing titanic explosions. As in a blast furnace, the burning coal reacted with ferrous iron (FeO) in the lava to form iron metal and carbon dioxide. Sulfur from the lava and coal added brimstone to the fire. Within days a broad area of Siberia became a monstrous landscape of collapsed pits and coal gas flares extending all the way into the stratosphere.

Overall, several trillion tons of carbon dioxide entered the atmosphere—the makings for a global disaster on land and sea. In comparison the atmosphere currently holds three trillion tons of carbon dioxide; doubling this amount would be calamitous.

The infernos continued for a decade, fed by the pool of lava at the base of the crust. Lava flows and coal fires continued for hundreds of thousands of years. Basalt flows eventually covered most of Siberia, a formation now known as the Siberian Traps.

Dreadful Aftermath

The initial effect of the Siberia coal fires on the climate was mild: a cold spring in the northern hemisphere, with a hazy sky. The smoke and dust settled, and sunlight once again reached the surface. But the heat could not escape through the new blanket of carbon dioxide and methane greenhouse gases. By summer, temperatures

were several degrees Celsius hotter than normal. Drought pre-
vailed. Plants withered and fungi prospered on the carcasses of
rotting plants and animals.

Seventy to seventy-five percent of the **"Trilobites wandered**
land species became extinct. **blindly to their**

Marine life suffered even more. Carbon **extinction."**
dioxide dissolved into the top sixty meters
of ocean water. The carbon dioxide and water created carbonic
acid, as happens in carbonated drinks (chemically: $CO_2 + H_2O \rightarrow$
H_2CO_3, carbonic acid.) Seawater became acidic. Calcium carbonate shells dissolved into a bicarbonate solution (chemically: $CaCO_3$
$+ H_2CO_3 \rightarrow Ca^{++} + 2HCO_3^-$). Shell-making organisms perished.
Reefs died. The food chain collapsed. Trilobites wandered blindly
to their extinction. The acid had dissolved the carbonate lenses of
their eyes.

Ninety-five percent of the marine species became extinct.

Mantle Plumes

What caused so much lava to erupt?

Modern geologists commonly ascribe the Siberia event to a
mantle plume starting near Earth's core. Tens of millions of years
before the eruption Earth's core heated the overlying mantle, and a
massive chunk of solid magma (yes, solid) slowly ascended through
the cooler mantle rock toward the surface. Scientific models of
mantle plumes resemble the flow of fluid in a lava lamp: The plume
has a long tail and a bulbous top, because the mantle flows more
quickly through the hot tail than the top can push its way up through
denser mantle.

Most but not all earth scientists accept mantle plumes. Seismologists have resolved their tail conduits in the uppermost few hundred kilometers. Images of the lower mantle (below seven hundred kilometers depth) show fuzzy features that may be tail conduits.

This huge bulb of mantle rose slowly, a few centimeters per year, and eventually reached the base of the lithosphere, the cool layer of rock near Earth's surface. Now under less pressure, it partially melted and spread out like a bubble beneath aquarium glass. Hot basalt lava began to flow upward through the crust to meet its fate with the coal.

Magma plumes are common in the geological record. The Palisades basalt near New York City is the result of an event two hundred million years ago. Giant's Causeway of the Spanish Armada's bane formed sixty million years ago. More than a dozen basalt plains are known, each caused by a hot mantle plume that originated near the core of the planet.

Philosophy

"Madness! To be enraged with a dumb thing, Captain Ahab, seems blasphemous."

—*Moby Dick* by Herman Melville (1819–1891)

We can do nothing to prevent mantle plumes. Starbuck rebukes Ahab, a prime fictional candidate for a Darwin Award, with the pragmatic Yankee view of natural phenomena as purposeless and uncaring. Charles Darwin quoted Aristotle, who said that rain falls not (with the intention) to ruin crops during harvest. If a mantle plume has a ticket to a coal or oil field, no prayers can swerve its course. But there is one consolation. Be assured that seismologists would have already detected the approach of such a mantle plume.

Science does not draw moral lessons from natural events, but one can make a practical analogy, and the analogy is stark. The herds of dicynodonts had no hand in the Great Dying, but we burn fossil fuels of our own volition. We know that burning fossil fuel puts heat and carbon dioxide into the air. About a third of the carbon dioxide now in our atmosphere was generated from this source. We have the power to avoid a man-made repeat of the great Permian extinctions by using other energy sources, or by sequestering the carbon dioxide we generate.

Our educational system has brought us to the realizations of Aristotle and Starbuck. Weather is regarded as a natural phenomenon beyond our control. Ironically, we must now teach the public that weather is no longer an immutable natural phenomenon. We are the masters of our climate.

We can learn from the distant past—or repeat it.

Norm Sleep teaches geophysics at Stanford University. His interests include conditions on Earth and the habitability of other planets. He was born in Kalamazoo, Michigan, and grew up in the paper mill town of Parchment. He graduated from Michigan State University and arrived at MIT during the plate-tectonic scientific revolution. His thesis was on subducting slabs. He taught at Northwestern University before moving to Stanford. His interest in habitability stems from his work on hydrothermal circulation at midoceanic ridges and his work on the feeble tectonic activity on Mars.

CHAPTER 7

COMBUSTION CRAZIES

Pyrotechnical allure seduces many a man to his untimely demise. So many combustibles to choose from: fireworks, grenades, flaming shots, elemental sodium, homemade bombs, and lightsabers. . . . In order to evolve traits that protect us against a fascination with the flammable, we must sacrifice a few limbs and lives.

Darwin Award: Electronic Fireworks

Confirmed True by Darwin

1 JANUARY 2007, NETHERLANDS

The first Darwin Award of 2007 went to Serge, thirty-six, who thought it reasonable to hover over an illegal professional firework and light the *electronic* ignition with an open flame. This was not a traditional fuse—it was a device designed for precision timing, and a flame should not have been used at all. Regardless of the fuse type a person's head should never be placed in the way of a firework.

The heat triggered an immediate launch and the firework catapulted upward, killing our amateur pyrotechnician en route to a spectacular burst across the night sky.

A witness told reporters, "His face disappeared. If someone has no face left, you know it's serious." Serge had purchased the firework legally in Belgium but then illegally transported it into the Netherlands. His father disputed the notion that Serge was careless, characterizing his son as a man who gave due consideration to his acts.

"If someone has no face left, you know it's serious."

Every year another idiot gets nominated for a Darwin Award for this same reason. Please, readers, keep your itchy fingers off the triggers of these dangerous fireworks!

Reference: fok.nl, ad.nl

Darwin Award: Rolling Stones

Confirmed True by Darwin

20 MARCH 2006, VIETNAM

A rolling stone is not all that gathers no moss. Three Vietnamese men scavenging for scrap metal found an unexploded five-hundred-pound bomb perched atop a hill near Hanoi and decided to retrieve it with a little help from Sir Isaac Newton. After all, gravity is free. As they rolled the bomb down the hillside, it detonated, blasting a four-meter crater and sending all three entrepreneurs to a face-to-face meeting with their deceased hero.

Reference: WISTV.com

Darwin Award: Hammer of Doom

Confirmed True by Darwin

AUGUST 2006, BRAZIL

Philosophy Corner

Darwin has begun to question the merits of landmine nominations. Many a poor person must take risks to put food on the table. A reader who cleared mines for many years said, "These people have little choice but to scavenge metal to feed their families. It's not stupid behavior, although many are killed. A sad state of affairs." When a poor person takes risks for his family, he is acting honorably. On the other hand, slamming a sledgehammer into a mine that is meant to blow a human being to smithereens is surely the least best way to salvage metal from it. Avoiding one's own demise is ALSO of use to the family.

What do you think?

darwinawards.com/darwin/
darwin2006-04.html

August brings us a winner from Brazil, who tried to disassemble a rocket-propelled grenade (RPG) by driving back and forth over it with a car. This technique was ineffective, so he escalated to pounding the RPG with a sledgehammer. The second try worked—in a sense. The explosion proved fatal to one man, six cars, and the repair shop wherein the efforts took place.

> **"This technique was ineffective, so he escalated. . . ."**

Fourteen more RPGs were found in a car parked nearby. Police believe the ammunition was being scavenged to sell as scrap metal. If it wasn't scrap then, it certainly is now!

Reference: WISTV.com, *O Dia* (Brazil), msnbc.com, UK *Daily Mail*

Reader Comments:

"Wham . . . wham . . . kaboom!"
"This is the hardest egg I ever had to crack!"
"More scrap metal than he planned for."

Darwin Award: Timing Is Everything

Confirmed True by Darwin

9 DECEMBER 2007, INDIANA

Russell, nineteen, had a grudge against a semitruck abandoned on a rural property. Russell was not the silent, brooding type. He was a man of action. He built a gunpowder-and-propane tank bomb, attached a timer, planted it in the moldering truck, and retreated to a distant vantage point to wait for the fireworks.

And waited.

And waited, until he could wait no more. No boom? This was not right. Why was nothing happening? Russell approached the stubborn truck—just in time for an up-close-and-personal look at a cloud of rapidly expanding incandescent gas.

"He waited. And waited. And waited until he could wait no more."

Detectives found bomb-making materials at Russell's mobile home and believe he was also responsible for two explosions the night before his death, one at the mobile home park and another at a hobby shop. Although Russell will be missed, we are all a bit safer now.

Reference: theindychannel.com; *The Indianapolis Star*; *The Star Press*, Muncie, IN

At Risk Survivor: The Flaming Shot

Unconfirmed

NOVEMBER 2001, MINNESOTA

Grain alcohol and fire don't mix.

After consuming many cocktails at a party, my friends and I had a BRILLIANT idea to pour a shot of ALCOHOL and set it on FIRE and drink it. I believe the ultimate goal was to impress the ladies present.

This excellent suggestion would be easy to accomplish since we had nearly pure grain alcohol in front of us. Let me add that the person who described the flaming shot neglected to mention that you are supposed to blow it out before swallowing it.

So we poured the liquor into a shot glass and set it on fire. So far, so good! We looked at each other, each hoping someone else would volunteer to be the guinea pig. After much debate we had our first contender. My friend proceeded to pick up the shot glass, put it down, pick it up, put it down, and finally he simply stared at the flames for a good two minutes.

> **"The ultimate goal was to impress the ladies present."**

"C'mon, man up!"

"?!$%!! that!" he declared.

I decided that the democratic process would produce no results. I picked up the hot glass and slammed the flaming concoction down my throat. Upside: The fire was quickly extinguished after I closed

my mouth. Downside: The inside of my mouth felt and tasted like it was burning. For two days.

I was too much in shock to speak.

The friend who had previously hesitated saw how easily the shot had been dispatched and prepared another for himself. Not to be outdone, he poured the grain alcohol right up to the rim of the glass and lit it. Upside: He would outdo me! Downside: Completely full shot glasses are difficult to lift without spilling. And if the liquor is on fire when it spills . . .

He proceeded to light his hand and the countertop on fire. Then, demonstrating that drinking does in fact reduce reaction time, he tried to stop drinking it but ended up pouring it on his face and sweatshirt. Upside: His goatee insulated his face from the fire. Downside: Hair is flammable. He caught on fire.

Most of his facial hair was burning by the time we stopped laughing long enough to realize he had no idea what to do. We extinguished the growing blaze by slapping him in the face with a kitchen towel. Fortunately for us, but less fortunately for the gene pool, this event did not qualify anyone for a Darwin Award.

Moral: Any feat involving fire and grain alcohol that is described as brilliant . . . isn't.

Reference: Eyewitness account by Colin Hammer

At Risk Survivor: Star Wars

Confirmed True by Darwin

2006, ENGLAND

Two people, seventeen and twenty, emulated Luke Skywalker and Darth Vader and fought each other with lightsabers. Only, they didn't have toy lightsabers, so they made their own from fluorescent lightbulbs. That's right, they each opened up a fluorescent tube, poured gasoline inside, and lit the bulb. As one can imagine, a Star Wars–sized explosion was not far behind. Both participants survived to confess to their creative, but stupid, film reenactment.

Darwin says: Seventeen is the legal driving age. Old enough to pump gas is old enough to know better than to light gasoline in a fluorescent tube.

Reference: BBC News, *Daily Telegraph*

Reader Comment:

"Maybe they should have stuck to the Dark Side."

At Risk Survivor: Unfinished Project
Unconfirmed

Any story that begins, "Well I was building a pipe bomb," can never end well. Lou is, on the surface, a bright and successful individual with an appetite for building new things. Things like axles and pipe bombs. One Sunday, bored and angry that the Broncos were losing, Lou decided to head to his basement workshop to try and build a bomb.

He welded a pipe closed on one end. Taking every precaution one can take when one is illegally creating high explosives, Lou was smart enough to let the metal cool before he put the powder into the pipe. When he was done packing the gunpowder, he realized that he had run out of welding rod. And so he set the half-finished pipe bomb on the scrap-metal heap for later.

"He forgot about the bomb project for six long months." Pipe bombs, like any other half-done task, have a tendency to stay undone for a great deal of time. That's what happened with Lou's project. He simply forgot about the pipe bomb for six long months, summer and fall.

A few days before hunting season Lou was loading his hunting gear into his pride-and-joy Ford Bronco, when he noticed that a shaft was cracked. Being an expert welder, he knew he could fix the cracked pipe himself. Need I say more?

Lou reached into his scrap-metal pile, pulled out a pipe, pulled down his welding hood, and struck an arc. He remembers a loud bang and not much else.

Shrapnel embedded itself up to the rafters of the third floor of his house! A piece of shrapnel even blew through Lou's welding hood, missing his empty skull by half an inch.

No good ever comes from the phrase "Well I was building a pipe bomb."

Reference: Eyewitness account by Mike

"We are all born ignorant but one must work hard to remain stupid."

—Benjamin Franklin

At Risk Survivor: Roundabout Rocket
Unconfirmed

Two teens were playing with miniature rockets that they had ac-
quired goodness-knows-where. Between the two of them the idea
was formed to tie a string around the rocket, tether it to the backyard birdbath, and thereby cause it to whirl around the sky. Since
no sturdy string was at hand, one had the brilliant idea to swipe
some freely available yarn from his mother.

The scheme was laid.

They lit the rocket and skittered back from the wheel of sparks
they expected. But their expectations were dashed. Instead of
watching the rocket spin around its tether, a different experience
was in store for them. The flame of the rocket propulsion quickly
burned through the yarn, and the rocket found a new trajectory
straight toward a vulnerable stomach.

The boy was alternately clutching his bruised gut in pain and
smacking his shirt to remove the rocket and extinguish the flames.
He came away from the experience with a large contusion and a
ruined, and hastily hidden, shirt. The boys never told their parents
what they had done.

Here's the kicker: They had graduated from high school the day
before! Heaven knows how.

Reference: Anonymous eyewitness account by a reader who says,
"The protagonist is my ex-boyfriend. I'm glad I am no longer in line to assist
in propagating his genes!"

At Risk Survivor:
Remember the *Hindenburg*
Unconfirmed

Remember science class? Remember the time the teacher dropped crystals of sodium into a bowl of water? Students watch in awe as the element skips about, fizzing as it burns. Well, for one teacher this tidy little demonstration didn't go exactly to plan.

A glass safety screen is usually placed between the bowl and the students so random bits of sodium don't jump out and scald them. This particular teacher decided to put the screen over the bowl, lifting it up to drop in sodium. He did this several times, so all the children could see. When he was done he removed the screen from the bowl.

$$2\,Na + 2\,H_2O = 2\,NaOH + H_2$$

Sodium in water produces hydrogen gas. And this teacher had the bad judgment to have a Bunsen burner burning near the edge of his desk. When he lifted the glass screen the accumulated hydrogen exploded!

The students were just leaving the classroom when they heard an almighty BANG. They turned back to see the teacher on his ass looking shell-shocked,

"They were picking bits out of the ceiling for a fortnight."

with bits of the overhead fluorescent lighting falling down from the ceiling. None of the students was hurt (except aches from laughing),

and the teacher really should have known better than to let hydrogen build up.

But that said, another teacher in the same department accidentally let a senior student make nitroglycerine. They were picking bits of lab equipment out of the ceiling for a fortnight. This submission only qualifies for an Honorable Mention since, despite their best efforts, these science teachers remain in the gene pool.

Reference: Anonymous eyewitness account

"It's not getting any smarter out there. You have to come to terms with stupidity, and make it work for you."

—Frank Zappa

At Risk Survivor: Hot Rod

Confirmed True by Darwin

29 JANUARY 2007, OREGON

At two-thirty A.M. a Volkswagen Jetta was hot-rodding down the interstate at speeds exceeding a hundred miles per hour. Suddenly the vehicle lost traction, cartwheeled, narrowly avoided a hundred-foot plunge into the Clackamas River, and smashed through the wall of a garage.

The unfortunate resident leapt out of bed in alarm and rushed down the hall and into the garage. A car was jammed halfway through the wall! It was resting on the passenger side, and the air was thick with gasoline fumes. And someone was rummaging around in the backseat!

"There's gas, there's gas!" the resident shouted.

"I need my knife," the figure yelled back. His knife? The figure flicked open a lighter, apparently the better to see. The flame jumped from the lighter to the backseat, from the backseat to the front, and the whole interior of the car was in flames!

A bold and heroic neighbor grabbed a fire extinguisher, shattered the back window, and sprayed inside. Just as the driver was pulled free through a rear window, the fumes exploded! The car kept burning until it was extinguished by professional firefighters.

The driver, twenty-two, was lucky to survive with minor burns. He was cited for driving under the influence with a suspended license.

After the excitement was over, the unfortunate residents of the apartment went to a friend's house for the remainder of the night. "We needed a nap."

Reference: *The Oregonian,* oregonlive.com

6 MARCH 2007, TEXAS

In a similar incident a flaming car crashed into a house in Waco. What happened? The vehicle had run out of gas earlier in the evening, and after replenishing the tank from a gas can, the driver tossed the "empty can" into the backseat. Later, while searching for the overturned gas can, he flicked a lighter . . . giving a new meaning to the term *hot rod.*

Since discretion is the better part of valor, the brave driver abandoned the burning car and watched as it rolled into a nearby house. One wonders just how he explained things to the homeowner. "I dropped the Olympic torch while delivering it to Beijing"?

Reference: *Waco Tribune-Herald*

At Risk Survivor: Helmet Head

Confirmed True by Darwin

12 AUGUST 2006, INDIANA

At a party somewhere between Nashville and Bloomington, a young man was drinking and watching people set off fireworks. Suddenly a great idea occurred to him. He could improve upon this amateur fireworks display! He put down his drink and set to work.

"He put down his drink and set to work." When it comes to fireworks, your brain can't be much safer than sheltered inside a football helmet. He found an old helmet, duct-taped a mortar-style firework to the top, put it on his head, and lit the fuse. . . .

A bright flash of light nearly blinded observers. When their eyes recovered, they saw him lying on the ground, unconscious and bleeding. Astoundingly, the twenty-one-year-old survived this party stunt with only a mild concussion and burns.

His helmet, however, was blown to pieces.

Reference: *Bloomington Herald-Times*, WSBT.com, Associated Press

Reader Comments:

"That sounds fun!"

"Fourth of July, Darwin-style."

Darwin Award: Garden Bomb

STATUS: Unconfirmed, Possible Urban Legend

2006, AUSTRALIA

In the suburbs of Adelaide, the "undisputed cannabis capital of Australia," sleeping residents were awakened by a resounding explosion. A smoking hole was found in a neighbor's backyard, still reeking of the pungent odor of marijuana. Police found the remains of a man at the bottom of the hole.

They learned that the deceased had set up a hidden hydroponic system in a large water tank buried in his backyard. He used a CO_2 generator—a small flame from a butane gas bottle—to improve plant growth. On this particular evening the man had climbed down into his garden paradise, only to find that the flame had gone out. Without knowing how many days the gas had been leaking into his, er, bomb, he relit the flame. . . .

> **"A smoking hole was found in the backyard, still reeking of marijuana."**

Darwin says: Is this an urban legend? I received many skeptical comments, including some from residents of Adelaide. I found a promising lead purporting to be an Australian police document from the relevant territorial force; however, their entire online media center is offline at present. The veracity of each story relies on reader input, so contact Darwin to confirm or refute: www .DarwinAwards.com/book/ contact.html

SCIENCE INTERLUDE:
THE HUMANITY

By Tom Arnold

Introduction

From the mind of J. R. R. Tolkien sprang legendary adventures of cunning warlocks, elegant Ents, monstrous Ringwraithes, sword-wielding heroes, beatific elves, and demonic villains. In 2001 they were brought to the big screen by the very real wizards of special effects, in a movie adaptation of *The Lord of the Rings*. These tales are considered sheer genius, unadulterated fun, and of course pure fantasy. But on the shores of a tiny island in the Pacific the ancient bones of a forgotten race lay buried in an Indonesian Middle Earth. A few years ago the fossils surfaced, and we realized Tolkien was right: Here there be Hobbits.

It struck the anthropological world like a lightning bolt: Anatomically modern humans, *Homo sapiens,* may have shared the planet with another human species as recently as twelve thousand years ago! Christened *Homo floresiensis*, or Flores Man, after the island on which it was discovered, the species is better known by the nickname "Hobbits."

Debate now rages over Australian archaeologist Mike Mor-

wood's 2003 discovery. Are Hobbits truly a separate human species, or merely an extreme variant of modern humans?

Meet the Hobbits

Skeletons and Artifacts

The Hobbits' skeletons and artifacts, ranging from 100,000 to
12,000 years old, present a confusing picture. They are perhaps
best described as miniature *Homo erectus*, a species that lived 1.8
million to 250,000 years ago. But the Hobbit tools found by archaeologists are a much older design. They are similar to Oldawan
flaked stone choppers used by *Australopithecus* 3 to 2.3 million
years ago, or tools used by *Homo habilis* 2.3 to 1.6 million years ago.
This discrepancy can be explained by a theory advanced by archaeologist Hallam Movius, who noticed that early prehistoric human
sites east of a line through northern India produced only Oldawan-
like chopper tools. One explanation is that *H. erectus* left Africa
before the development of hand-ax technology. The Hobbits apparently hunted game, including pygmy elephant and giant rat, using
these unsophisticated flaked stone choppers.

Hobbit Brains

The undisputed Hobbit celebrity is a nearly complete skull of a
middle-aged female, known affectionately as "Flo." Flo's skull, like
those of the other skeletons, is small. But the fact that these petite
primates made stone tools and hunted large game suggests that
their mental capacity was not small.

To shed light on this puzzle, the discrepancy between brain size and apparent intelligence, scientists sought more information about Hobbit brains. Brains are soft tissue, but their surface features sometimes leave impressions inside the skull. Those surface features reveal a lot about brain structure and complexity. So endocasts, three-dimensional models of that interior, are often created to examine brain surface features.

Hobbit skulls were too fragile for traditional plaster casts, so a virtual endocast based on a CT scan was created by Dean Falk of Florida State University. Although the size of the brain was as small as a modern chimp's, the shape was similar to that of *H. erectus erectus*. Of particular interest in the Hobbit brain was the enlargement of Brodmann's area 10, which in modern humans is associated with planning.

Hobbits Only Recently Extinct

Unlike earlier hominid populations that disappeared when modern humans arrived, the Hobbit population may well have survived and coexisted with modern humans. Local island folklore describes the *ebu gogo*, a small creature that lived in the jungle, had a huge appetite, a limping walk, and spoke in a quiet, indistinct fashion. Could the folklore preserve a cultural memory of another human species? According to fossils evidence Morwood's Hobbits disappeared about the time a local volcano erupted twelve thousand years ago. The eruption may have destroyed their habitat, or perhaps the Hobbits were caught unawares and, like Pompeii citizens, quickly engulfed by the eruption.

The discovery of a Hobbit shire complete with Hobbit bones,

brains, and tools might seem to be conclusive evidence for the existence of these little people. But that is not how science works. The discovery challenges previously held theories that must be reconciled with the new data. The resulting scientific debates make a battle with Orcs seem tame by comparison.

Controversial Implication: We Were Not Alone

So why does the discovery of Hobbits intrigue archaeologists and paleoanthropologists? Prior to this discovery it was thought that humans have not shared the planet with another species of the genus *Homo* since 30,000 years before the founding of Rome. Modern humans and Neanderthals genetically diverged about 450,000 years ago. When Neanderthals (*Homo neanderthalensis* or *Homo sapiens neanderthalensis*) died out (or were absorbed into the European population) 33,000 years ago, archaeological evidence indicates that we became the sole winner of a two-million-year *Survivor* competition against all other *Homo* species, such as *Homo habilis* and *Homo erectus*.

If the Hobbit hypotheses proposed by Morwood's team are accurate, this widely accepted story will need to be rewritten. Since the field is fraught with contradictory evidence and conflicting scientific opinions, it will not be easy to rewrite the human story.

Ancestors of Humans

Paleoanthropologists by and large agree that *Homo ergaster*, an early form of *H. erectus* found in Africa, is the earliest direct ancestor to anatomically modern humans. Later *H. erectus* remains found outside of Africa are thought to represent an offshoot—an evolutionary dead end—rather than a link to modern humans, but this is still hotly debated.

It is also widely agreed that *Homo erectus*, as a distinct species, existed from 1.8 million years ago to about 250,000 years ago, with the Indonesian fossils dating from 1.6 million to 700,000 years ago. More recent finds, however, indicate that *Homo erectus* may have been living on Java less than 100,000 years ago. The latter dates would bolster the interpretations of Morwood and his colleagues.

Ancestors of Hobbits

Several fossil species have been suggested as the ancestors of the Hobbits. These include *Homo habilis*, Handy Man, or the ancient *Australopithecus*, of which Lucy is the most famous specimen. Until recently these ancestors seemed unlikely, because there was no evidence that either species had left Africa. However, recent finds in the Republic of Georgia indicate that a small tool-making hominid may have left Africa as early as 1.7 million years ago.

Controversy

The field of human evolution is a minefield of contentious opinions. Since the subject of human origins is emotional, bragging rights over who has discovered our oldest direct ancestor (the legendary missing link) can bring fame if not fortune to the discoverers. New discoveries and potentially new species can upset long-held views that earlier researchers had developed careers and reputations on. Thus, the Hobbit discovery was quickly dismissed by some paleoanthropologists as improbable. Perhaps they are the remains of modern humans suffering from microcephaly, a genetic disorder that causes a skull deformity and mental retardation. Others have suggested that the remains represent modern humans suffering from a deficiency in iodine and selenium, and a diet of cyanide-rich foods such as cassava.

These notions have been dismissed by the Australian team who discovered the fossils. The detractors did not have access to the original fossils or casts, and they contended that it is not credible that a group of physically and mentally deformed people survived and successfully hunted game for nearly a hundred thousand years.

Mike Morwood cites the principle of island dwarfism to explain the small size of the fossils. Once on the island the isolated population would have begun to

Island Dwarfism

In an isolated environment with limited resources the slow scalpel of natural selection speeds to a ruthless blur. Large social mammals such as mammoths or rhinoceroses grow smaller because the efficiency of small size offers a powerful adaptive advantage. Conversely, small animals such as birds, lizards, and rats may become quite large without the selective pressure of traditional predators. Which animals will grow large or shrink depends on a complex combination of factors.

evolve along its own trajectory, guided by regional conditions. One of these changes was shrinkage in their physical stature. On the island of Flores island dwarfism also affected a species of elephant that shrank in size and a species of rat that grew larger.

Sadly, the Hobbit remains were caught up in a petty dispute by anthropologists who disagreed with Morwood's interpretation. When the specimens were recovered, key pelvis and jawbones were damaged and contaminated with modern human DNA.

With many questions still unanswered, public interest waned.

Controversy over early hominid remains have a long association with Indonesia. Java Man, cousin to Peking Man, was found in 1891 on the Indonesian island of Java by the Dutch physician Eugène Dubois. On returning to Europe he exhibited his finds, claiming he had found the "missing link" between humans and apes. However, Dubois's claims were not widely accepted. He became resentful and eventually refused to show the fossils to anyone.

Another Dwarf Hominid!

Then lightning struck again! In 2008 on the island nation of Palau, not far from Flores, another group of dwarf hominids was unearthed. The "Palau Pygmies" appear to be anatomically much closer to modern humans than the comparatively small-brained Hobbits from Flores. They were also tiny—a little over one meter tall and weighing roughly seventy pounds. Even more stunning, the new remains date back only a couple of thousand years! Based on the limited information released to date our genetic cousins may have been running around on one side of the world, while the Roman Empire rose and fell on the other.

The Profound Question of Humanity

Both discoveries bring up profound questions about what it is to be human. Today we struggle with the definition of human life at a fundamental level. Rival camps argue whether a fetus, a blastocyst, or a fertilized egg should be guaranteed the full rights of a person. What if creatures similar to the Palau Pygmies and Flores Hobbits are found to exist in isolated jungle pockets? Should they be displayed in zoos? Put to medical or experimental uses? Protected in their native environment as rare and endangered species? Liberated from their stone age existence? And what if the Flores Hobbits *evolved from modern humans*, as some researchers suspect? That would make *Homo sapiens* the transitional species.

Paradoxically, answering the question of whether the Hobbits and Palau Pygmies are human might teach us more about our own humanity than the humanity of the island dwarves.

Additional Reading:

Morwood, Mike, and Penny van Oosterzee, *A New Human: The Startling Discovery and Strange Story of the "Hobbits" of Flores, Indonesia*. New York: HarperCollins, 2004.

Wong, Kate, 2006. The littlest human. In *Becoming Human: Evolution and the Rise of Intelligence*. *Scientific American* Special Edition. Vol. 16, No. 2: 48–57.

Tom Arnold (no Roseanne jokes, please, I've heard them all) has a Ph.D. in archaeology from Simon Fraser University. Tom currently lives in London, Ontario, Canada, trying to earn a living working in consulting archaeology. His aged mother would like him to find a real job/career whenever he decides to grow up.

CHAPTER 8

ANIMAL ANTICS

We may think we rule the planet, but Mother Nature is the real boss. Tigers, cows, moles, bears, rabbits, fish, elephants, bees, buffalo, snakes, sharks, a dog, and a deer . . . animals can, and do, use their instinctive wiles to "out" clueless *Homo sapiens*. Moo!

Darwin Award: Kittie Toy

Confirmed True by Darwin

18 DECEMBER 2005, SOUTH AFRICA

Two muggers were working a crowd at the zoo. They had just taken a cell phone and purse from a couple at knifepoint when suddenly, the woman screamed. The muggers sprinted away.

But working a crowd and working out are entirely different activities, and one of the muggers was out of shape.

"I don't have to outrun that tiger; I just have to outrun you." As he watched his compatriot recede into the distance, he felt the stitch in his side and knew he could run no farther. Perhaps he was thinking he should have spent some of those ill-gotten gains on a trip to the gym. But then he spotted a high fence, and that, at least, he could manage.

He put on a burst of speed and leapt the fence. Sure enough, no one followed. Escape! But he had failed to take into consideration a very important fact. He was at the Bloemfontein Zoo. Just as he was congratulating himself on his foolproof escape, he realized that on the other side of the fence was a ten-meter drop into a cage of bored Bengal tigers.

Speaking of foolproof, the tigers wasted no time in treating the nearest fool as their own little kitty toy. The mauled body of the mugger was not noticed until noon. A zoo spokesperson said that it was lucky the tigers had been fed the previous afternoon, else they would have left no evidence behind.

Police said a postmortem would be carried out to determine the exact cause of his death—as if that wasn't obvious.

Reference: *Die Volksblad,* news24.com

Reader Comment:
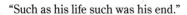

"Crime pays for the tigers' just desserts."

"Such as his life such was his end."

—Corgrave's 1611 French/English Dictionary

Darwin Award: Whac-A-Mole

Confirmed True by Darwin

10 JANUARY 2007, EAST GERMANY

A sixty-three-year-old man's extraordinary effort to eradicate moles from his property resulted in a victory for the moles. The man pounded several metal rods into the ground and connected them—not to household current, which would have been bad enough—but to a *high-voltage* power line, intending to render the subterranean realm uninhabitable.

Incidentally, the maneuver electrified the very ground on which he stood. He was found dead some time later, at his holiday property on the Baltic Sea. Police had to trip the main circuit breaker before venturing onto the property.

The precise date of the sexagenarian's demise could not be ascertained, but the electric bill may provide a clue.

Reference: *Der Spiegel* (Germany), Reuters (Berlin)

Reader Comment:

"Think this would work for squirrels?
I wouldn't have a problem with them anymore.
I wouldn't have a problem with anything."

Darwin Award: Beer for Bears

Confirmed True by Darwin

19 AUGUST 2007, SERBIA

It's well known that alcohol impairs judgment. It's well known that carnivorous wild animals and humans don't mix. What happens when we combine all three? One might expect men, beer, and bears to combine with lethal consequences. Such was the case for a twenty-three-year-old man who inadvertently fed himself to Masha and Misha at the Belgrade Zoo.

The zoo director said of the incident, "Only an idiot would jump into the bear cage."

The man's naked, mauled corpse was found inside the bear habitat, along with plenty of beer cans. His clothes were completely untouched, suggesting that he approached the bears bare-naked by choice.

> **The zoo director said, "Only an idiot would jump into the bear cage."**

The bears, apparently fearing that his intentions were as dishonorable as they were ill-informed, meted out a summary justice.

Later, Masha and Misha "reacted angrily" when keepers tried to recover the man's corpse, but were eventually persuaded to give up their bare prize. We await word on how many beers were bartered for the body.

Reference: CNN, Reuters

Reader Comments:

"Today's the day the teddy bears have their piiiiic-nic."
"Guess the guy misunderstood when his friend said,
'Hey, man, go git us a couple of dem beers.'"

"Some humans would do anything to see if it was possible.
If you put a large switch in a cave somewhere, with a sign
saying END OF THE WORLD SWITCH—PLEASE DO NOT TOUCH, the
paint wouldn't even have time to dry."

—Terry Pratchett, *Thief of Time*

Darwin Award: A Cow-ardly Death

Confirmed True by Darwin

19 APRIL 2007, CAMBODIA

Unwanted amorous advances on a heifer resulted in a man's death at the hooves of the violated bovine. Sounds of a scuffle culminated in the discovery of his naked body lying beneath the frightened family cow. Injuries were consistent with being kicked to death.

Why did he do it?

The man's divorce had become final ten days prior to his fateful final fling. In the divorce, and also a previous one, his ex-wives cited his insatiable desire as the cause of the divorce.

Phnom Penh police concluded that the man died in a rape gone wrong. They do not plan to take action against the cow, which appeared to have been acting in self-defense.

Reference: iol.co.za, Sapa-DPA

Reader Comments:

"That man loves his beef."

"No bull."

"Cow—boy."

"One last ride."

"A different way of 'getting the milk for free.'"

Darwin Award: Wascally Wabbit

Unconfirmed

Snowmobiles and alcohol are a dangerous mix. Then came the rabbit.

After a day spent partying and racing snowmobiles in the wilderness, a group of snowmobilers were headed back to their cabin, when up popped a jackrabbit! They gave chase. Several collisions were narrowly averted, so all the snowmobiles backed off . . . except one.

This snowmobiler kept his eye on the quarry and rapidly closed in. The rabbit darted aside to save itself. The snowmobiler closed in again. The rabbit ran toward the road, where there was less snow. Trying to ram his rabbit before it crossed the road, the man accelerated to Mach 1.

But the rabbit had other ideas. It darted into a culvert beneath the road. Witnesses stated that the snowmobiler never even braked. There was a metallic crunch as the accelerating vehicle rammed into the culvert, followed by a blast that shattered the snowmobile into a thousand bits.

This brand of snowmobile had a fuel tank mounted in front. The culvert admitted the tip of the snowmobile, then cut into the cowling, spilling fuel over the hot engine. The body of the ex-snowmobiler was blown twenty feet back into the field.

The rabbit's whereabouts were unknown.

Reference: Eyewitness account from an anonymous M.D.
with thirty years in the ER

Reader Comments:

"Hare Today, Gone Tomorrow"
"Kill the wabbit, kill the wabbit . . ."
"Wabbit: 1. Suicidal Idiot: 0."

"Don't approach a goat from the front, a horse from the
back, or a fool from any side."

—Jewish proverb

Darwin Award: Score One for Goliath

Confirmed True by Darwin

9 SEPTEMBER 2006, FLORIDA

The one that didn't get away.

A fearsome mythical giant named Goliath was felled by David's humble slingshot. But a modern leviathan versus a speargun is another tale altogether, as forty-two-year-old Gary discovered.

Although it was outlawed in 1990, poaching giant groupers remains surprisingly popular in the Florida Keys. These muscular fish can weigh six hundred pounds, yet underwater hunters voluntarily choose to tether themselves to the creatures with spearguns, in defiance of both the law and common sense.

Of this elite group our Darwin Award winner further distinguished himself by disregarding one essential spearfishing precaution. The "fit and experienced snorkeler" embarked on a grouper hunt without a knife to cut himself loose, guaranteeing that his next attack would be his last. "Not wearing a knife is like crossing I-95 with your eyes closed," explained one experienced diver.

The Goliath grouper is the world's largest grouper, attaining weights up to six hundred pounds. They are quite illegal to hunt and are generally too tough and wormy to eat, so killing one gives the spearfisher bragging rights only.

In those final hours the tables were turned, and the leviathan fish was given an opportunity to experience "catching a person." The body of the spearfisher was found pinned to the coral, seventeen feet underwater. Three coils of line were wrapped around his wrist, and one very dead grouper was impaled at the other end of the line.

Reference: *The Miami Herald*, Reuters, Yahoo! News

Reader Comments:

"Fish Catches Man Story"
"Sounds fishy to me."
"A reel fish tale."

Darwin Award: Elephants Press Back

Confirmed True by Darwin

2007, INDIA

Increased mining and heavy rains in southeast India have unsettled the wildlife. In recent months migrating elephants have killed eleven people. A team of four journalists decided to interview this herd of rogue elephants. They went into the forest in search of the rogues—on foot.

Elephants are big, and elephants are fast. As the recent deaths illustrate, a person can't outrun an elephant. But these intrepid journalists apparently assumed that a press pass grants immunity.

With a nose for news the journalists sniffed out the herd. Once located it was only natural to capture the photogenic animals on film. Unfortunately, the elephants were camera-shy. Angered by the flash, the irritated herd charged the paparazzi, miraculously killing only one of the four.

His remains could not be retrieved.

Reference: Hindu.com, NewIndPress.com

Darwin Award: Pulling a Boner!

Confirmed True by Darwin

2 FEBRUARY 2008, NEW YORK

A fifty-year-old man was bird-hunting in upstate New York with his buddies and his faithful canine companion. They stopped for a smoke, and his dog wandered off and found a deer leg bone.

The man tried to take the bone away, but like any right-thinking dog, the animal would not relinquish its treasure and stayed just out of reach. Frustrated with this blatant show of disobedience, the man grabbed his loaded shotgun by the muzzle and began wielding it like a club. Each time he swung it, the dog dodged.

Suddenly the "club" struck the ground and fired, shooting the man in the abdomen. He was airlifted to a nearby hospital, where he died from his injuries. He did remain conscious long enough to confirm this account to police; otherwise, his poor friends might now be under suspicion!

At least he didn't hit the dog.

Reference: Eyewitness account of a man who called 911, and recordonline.com

At Risk Survivor: Catching a Buzz
Unconfirmed

I work in a geology lab with very smart people. Charles can tell you the petrogenetic* peculiarities of low-alkali tholeiitic basalt after hydrothermal alteration, but our hero Charles recently demonstrated that there is a significant difference between intelligence and common sense.

While he was casting about for ways to rid himself of a pesky wasp nest, his eye fell upon his trusty Dirt Devil vacuum cleaner. Armed with this fearsome weapon, Charles attacked the wasp nest. He sucked up all the wasps, who buzzed angrily as they struggled in vain against the wind tunnel. The dust bag was soon alive with their buzzing.

Charles now found that he had a new problem: to wit, a vacuum cleaner bag full of live, disgruntled wasps. He had to find a way to kill them before he could safely turn off the vacuum. And while his previous idea was merely ill-considered, his next was a moronic masterpiece.

He held the vacuum tube in one hand, a can of Raid in the other, and proceeded to spray the insecticide into the vacuum. What our smart, young scientist failed to remember is that aerosols are flammable, and vacuum cleaner motors generate heat. The resulting explosion removed his facial hair and scattered the dusty, angry contents of the Dirt Devil all over the vicinity.

---

* Petrogenesis is the branch of science that deals with the origin and formation of rocks, especially igneous rock.

Adding insult to injury, Charles was not the only one to survive with minor injuries. The wasps proceeded to vent their spleen upon the exposed (and slightly scorched) skin of the scientist, who referred to the episode as "an unfortunate lapse in the calculation of consequences."

Reference: Anonymous eyewitness account

Reader Comments:

"Of Wasps and Men"
"No good deed goes uns(t)ung."

At Risk Survivor: Buffalo Stampede

Unconfirmed

1985

On my second day at Yellowstone National Park I rose early to get a good start on sightseeing. My second stop was a roadside parking lot near an open field where wild buffalo graze. The parking lot is lined with explicit warning signs. Buffalo are dangerous. Visitors should not leave their cars, and certainly not enter the field on foot.

I was taking snapshots with my telephoto lens when a car from California pulled in. A man with a camera emerged from the car. I heard him tell his wife that the buffalo were too far away, and he was going to walk out for a better shot. I called over, "Read the warning signs! Stay away from the animals."

He said nothing that big could catch him, and he walked to within fifty feet of a buffalo. I picked up the mike on my CB radio and started calling for the park rangers to bring a body bag.

As soon as his camera shutter clicked, the buffalo charged. Buffalo can run thirty-five miles per hour for short distances, so I was amazed that this man was able to sprint fifty yards back to his car ahead of the angry animal. He slid to a stop and managed to get in the car before the buffalo caught up.

"As soon as his camera shutter clicked, the buffalo charged."

But his car didn't escape the buffalo's attention. It rammed the car repeatedly, severely damaging the door, top, hood, radiator, lights, et cetera. The car was totaled. Park rangers arrived expecting a bloody mess, but the man and his wife survived with little more than glass cuts and, I suspect, some rather interesting marks in their undershorts.

Reference: Anonymous eyewitness account

"Life is tough, but it's tougher when you're stupid."

—John Wayne

At Risk Survivor: A Salty Tale

Unconfirmed

SEPTEMBER 1998, IDAHO

A few people out cow-tipping made so much noise that they woke the farmer. The farmer came running out with a shotgun loaded with rock salt, yelling "Get out of my fields!" One interloper yielded to an impulse to drop his pants and moon the farmer, offering a bright target in the dark night. The farmer took aim with his shotgun and pegged him in his butt and testicles!

The wounded man managed to crawl back to his car, where his snickering friends awaited. He was in great distress, but also in great embarrassment, and refused to go to the emergency room. His friends dropped him off at home, where he made the painful choice to soak the rock salt out in the tub.

Eight hours later, the young man was still unsuccessful. By then his parents had heard his muffled cries of agony and wondered what was up. When he finally admitted the truth, they rushed him to the emergency room, where doctors removed several chunks of salt and, from what I understand,

Cow-tipping is an activity in which members of our species attempt to prove their superiority over a "lesser" species by sneaking up on an unsuspecting cow sleeping on a hillside, and pushing her over. Laughter ensues among the triumphant humans as the "inferior" animal rolls down the hill, trying to regain its footing.

had the best laugh. One doctor told his parents that he would never be able to reproduce.

Reference: Idaho Falls *Post Register* and an anonymous eyewitness account

"No drug, not even alcohol, causes the fundamental ills of society. If we're looking for the source of our troubles, we shouldn't test people for drugs. We should test them for stupidity."

—P. J. O'Rourke

At Risk Survivor: Snake in the Grass

Confirmed True by Darwin

SCOTLAND

A biting story from Scotland.

Black adders are melanistic adders, not a species in their own right. Adders are normally greenish, with a black diamond pattern along their backs.

A hiker in Scotland picked up a harmless grass snake so his brother could take a picture. Just as he reached for it, a black adder slithered into view, so he grabbed that one too. The adder is Britain's only venomous snake. Both serpents sank their fangs into the forty-four-year-old, who responded with serious anaphylactic shock. He gradually and painfully recovered in the hospital. His excuse for his rash act? *He didn't think venomous snakes inhabited Scotland.*

Reference: *The Scotsman*

At Risk Survivor: "Bite Me!"

Confirmed True by Darwin

AUGUST 2007, OREGON

Man sticks rattlesnake in mouth to prove a point.

An amateur snake collector caught a twenty-inch rattlesnake on the highway. Three weeks later, his captive took its revenge. The formerly fearless snake charmer admitted, "You can assume alcohol was involved."

He had a six-pack under his belt and was consuming what he described as "a mixture of stupid stuff" at a barbecue.

"It's a nice snake. Nothing can happen."

The calamity was precipitated when he handed a beer to his ex, using the same hand that held the rattlesnake.

"Get that thing out of my face," she said.

He protested, "It's a nice snake. Nothing can happen. Watch!" Famous last words. As they left his mouth, his fate was sealed.

One month later, still sore from muscle and nerve damage from the venom, the twenty-three-year-old admitted that he stuck the snake in his mouth to prove his point. Instead, he disproved his point, for the snake bit him. He had no time for embarrassment over his mistake. In great pain and gasping for breath, he asked his ex to drive him to the hospital. "She was the only one sober," he explained.

He was unconscious by the time he arrived, his swollen tongue

protruding from his mouth. Physicians performed a tracheotomy to restore airflow to his lungs and administered antivenin. He was kept heavily sedated for several days. When the swelling went down, "we let him wake up," his doctor reported.

The Poison Control Center sees about fifty snakebite victims a year. Generally, they are injected on the legs while hiking, or arms while reaching under a rock. Few are bitten on the tongue.

His friends were blunt: "What the heck were you thinking?"

His answer? "It's my own stupidity."

Reference: *The Oregonian*, Associated Press, LiveScience.com

Reader Comments:

"Snake got your tongue?"
"Anyone wanna do SNAKE SHOTS?"

At Risk Survivor: Shark Kiss

Confirmed True by Darwin

AUGUST 2006, FLORIDA

A scuba diver was bitten on the lip when he attempted to kiss a nurse shark. The bite was a surprise to the diver, as he had kissed hundreds of sharks! He explained, "You pick 'em up, rub their belly, scratch 'em, hug 'em, might as well give them a smooch while you're there."

"The diver had kissed hundreds of sharks."

Past performance is no guarantee of future results. This shark took exception to his unwanted advances and bit the diver's lip. To add insult to injury, a group of snappers came in for a few nibbles too. Luckily, a patient plastic surgeon was able to repair his mangled lip.

"It was a matter of completing the puzzle and putting [a hundred little pieces] back together again," Dr. Mike Kelly said.

Has the diver learned his lesson? Apparently not! He simply plans to modify his amorous technique: "Don't kiss a nurse shark while it's *upside down*."

One reporter remarked, "Better still, don't kiss them at all."

Reference: CBS, divester.com

Urban Legend: Roping a Deer
STATUS: Urban Legend

Darwin warns: I cannot find an original source, nor any confirmation. Snopes.com has not yet addressed this story's veracity; however, its widespread presence on the Internet and its fantastical tone led me to consider the story a fabrication.

I had this idea that I was going to rope a deer, put it in a stall, sweet-feed it corn for a few weeks, then butcher it and eat it. Corn-fed venison. Yum! The first step in this culinary adventure was catching a deer.

Since they congregate at my cattle feeder and do not have much fear of me (a bold one will sometimes come right up and sniff at the bags of feed while I am in the back of the truck four feet away), it should not be difficult to rope one, toss a bag over its head to calm it down, then hog-tie it and transport it home.

I filled the cattle feeder and hid behind it with my rope. The cattle, having seen a roping or two before, stayed well back. They were not having any of it.

After twenty minutes my deer showed up, three of them. I picked a likely looking one, stepped out, and threw my rope. The deer just stood there and stared at me. I wrapped the rope around my waist and twisted the end so I would have a good hold. The deer still just stood and stared at me, but you could tell it was mildly concerned about the whole rope situation.

I took a step toward it. It took a step away. I put a little tension on

the rope and received an education. The first thing I learned is that, while a deer may just stand there looking at you funny while you rope it, it is spurred to action when you start pulling on that rope.

That deer EXPLODED.

The second thing I learned is that, pound for pound, a deer is a LOT stronger than a cow or a colt. A cow or a colt in that weight range, I could fight down with some dignity. A deer? No chance.

That thing ran and bucked, it twisted and pulled. There was no controlling that deer, and certainly no getting close to it. As it jerked me off my feet and started dragging me across the ground, it occurred to me that having a deer firmly attached to a rope was not such a good idea. The only upside is that they do not have much stamina.

> **"Deer are like horses, only twice as strong and three times as evil."**

A brief ten minutes later it was tired and not as quick to jerk me off my feet and drag me. It took me a few minutes to realize this, since I was mostly blinded by the blood flowing out of the big gash in my head.

At that point I had lost my appetite for corn-fed venison. I hated the thing and would hazard a guess that the feeling was mutual. I just wanted to get that devil creature off the end of that rope. But if I let it go with the rope hanging around its neck, it would likely die slow and painful somewhere.

Despite the gash in my head, and several large knots where I had cleverly arrested the deer's pell-mell flight by bracing my head against large rocks as it dragged me across the ground, I could still think clearly enough to recognize that I shared some tiny amount of responsibility for the situation we were in. I didn't want the deer to suffer a slow death.

I managed to get it lined up between my truck and the feeder, a little trap I had set beforehand, like a squeeze chute. I backed it in there, and I started moving forward to get my rope back.

Did you know that deer bite? They do!

I never in a million years would have thought that a deer would bite, so I was very surprised when I reached up there to grab hold of that rope, and the deer grabbed hold of my wrist. Now, when a deer bites you, it is not like a horse; it does not just bite and release. A deer bites and shakes its head, like a pit bull. They bite HARD and won't let go. It hurts!

The proper reaction when a deer bites you is probably to freeze and draw back slowly. I tried screaming and wrenching away. My method was ineffective. It felt like that deer bit and shook me for several minutes, but it was likely only several seconds.

I, being smarter than a deer (though you may be questioning that claim by now), tricked it. While I kept it busy tearing the bejesus out of my right arm, I reached up with my left hand and pulled that rope loose. That was when I learned my final lesson in deer behavior for the day.

Deer will strike at you with their front feet. They rear right up and strike at head and shoulder level, and their hooves are surprisingly sharp. I learned long ago that when a horse strikes at you with its hooves and you can't get away, the best thing to do is make a loud noise and move aggressively toward the animal. This will cause it to back down a bit, so you can make your escape.

This was not a horse. This was a deer. Obviously, such trickery would not work. In the course of a millisecond I devised a different strategy. I screamed like a child and turned to run.

The reason we have been taught NOT to turn and run from a horse that paws at you is that there is a good chance that it will hit you in the back of the head. Deer are not so different from horses after all, other than being twice as strong and three times as evil. The second I turned to run, it hit me right in the back of the head and knocked me down.

> Reader comment: "Roping a deer (or grabbing a wounded deer by the horns) may seem outrageous, but it has been done! And the deer don't like it at all. This kind of foolishness happens frequently. How do I know? I live in north-central Montana, and I tried to rope a deer myself once, but I missed. Thankfully. Deer are savage animals when trapped."

When a deer paws at you and knocks you down, it does not immediately depart. I suspect it does not recognize that the danger has passed. What it does instead is paw your back and jump up and down on you, while you are lying there crying like a baby and covering your head.

I finally managed to crawl under the truck, and the deer went away. Now I know why people go deer hunting with a rifle and a scope. It's so they can be somewhat equal to the prey.

Reference: Numerous Internet sources, none with attribution

CHAPTER 9

FAQ

FAQ: Why is it called the Darwin Awards?

Sorry you're dead, but thanks for not reproducing!
Here's a Darwin Award for your noble sacrifice.

—Wendy

The Darwin Awards are named in honor of Charles Darwin, a scientist fondly referred to as the father of evolution. The premise of the Awards is that the human species is still evolving. How do we know? We observe that people sometimes die due to their own brainless calculations. We hypothesize that there was something genetic behind the idiocy, something that would have been passed on to offspring. And we conclude that the next generation is one idiot smarter. If the human race is growing smarter over time, Charles Darwin would call that evolution!

FAQ: Is *this* a Darwin Award? The Rules.

People confide the most astonishing stories and ask, "Is *this* a Darwin Award?" There are more Darwin Awards and At Risk Survivors than I can possibly chronicle. Decide for yourself using this handy Field Guide to Identifying a Darwin Award.

Field Guide to Identifying a Darwin Award

To win, an adult must eliminate herself from the gene pool in an astonishingly stupid way that is verifiably true.

Reproductive dead end: Out of the gene pool

The Darwin Awards poke ironic fun at the self-removal of incompetent genes from the human race. The potential winner must therefore render herself deceased or, more happily, still alive but incapable of reproducing (nudge, wink). If someone does manage to survive an incredibly stupid feat, then her genes ipso facto have something to offer in the way of luck, agility, or stamina. She is therefore not eligible for a Darwin Award, though sometimes the story is too entertaining to pass up and the At Risk Survivor earns an honorable mention.

Excellence

The true Darwin Award winner exhibits an astounding lack of judgment. We are not talking about common mishaps like breaking a leg while skiing. The final fatal act must be of truly idiotic magnitude, like sledding down a ski run on foam protective padding you recently removed from the ski towers (page 141).

The Darwin Award winner overlooks risks that are seemingly impossible to overlook. Baking bullets in an oven, driving while reading, using the butt end of a loaded rifle as a club, taking the batteries out of the carbon monoxide detector because the alarm keeps going off. . . . that sort of thing. "What were they thinking?"

Self-selection: The candidate caused her own demise.

Nobody can give you a Darwin Award. You have to earn your own by showing a gross ineptitude for survival. A driver hit by a falling tree is a victim of circumstance. If you roped the tree to your pickup (page 108) . . . you are a candidate for a Darwin Award.

However, if you are intentionally attempting to win, you are disqualified! I do not want to encourage risk-taking behavior. Most extreme sports accidents are also disqualified, because the person made a willing trade-off between risk and reward.

Maturity: The candidate is not a kid, or otherwise handicapped.

Nobody laughs when a child dies. Anyone below the age of sixteen does not qualify. A child does not possess sufficient maturity and experience to make life-or-death decisions, and the responsibility

for her safety still resides with her guardians. Similarly, the death of a person with physical or mental handicaps is not amusing if it results from an innate impediment, rather than a poor decision. Those who lack maturity are not eligible for an Award.

Veracity: The event is true.

If it happened to you, you know it's true. Otherwise, rely on reputable newspapers (not *Weekly Whirled News*) or other published articles, confirmed television reports, and so forth. Responsible eyewitnesses are also valid sources, particularly if there are several independent confirmations. Be warned, though! What your brother says is probably true. What your brother said his friend's boss said is not reliable! Nor is a chain e-mail or a doctored photograph. The use of your own "bullshit radar" is highly recommended. It's probably more accurate than you realize. Also a quick reality check with www.Snopes.com can sort the wheat from the chaff, the legend from the likely.

FAQ: I already have kids. Am I safe?

Yes. You passed your genes along. You're safe!

The broader question is whether a person with offspring can win a Darwin Award. Our community engages in interminable and ultimately inconclusive discussions about what it means to be out of the gene pool. What if the winner has already reproduced? What if the nominee has an identical twin? Old people aren't going to have any (more) kids—are old people disqualified? What about cryogenics: frozen sperm and eggs? If cloning humans becomes possible, will Darwin Awards cease to exist?

And the answer is . . . I don't know. These questions are vexing. But if you no longer have the physical wherewithal to breed with a mate on a desert island, you are eligible for a Darwin Award.

FAQ: Sometimes the winners are still alive?!

True. Some aren't dead. Some are sterile! Men who carry a loaded gun (page 114) in the waistband of their trousers, men who survive an amorous encounter with a vacuum cleaner or porcupine—a few lucky "winners" are out of the gene pool, yet still alive to collect their Awards in person.

Also you will read another type of story in the book. Darwin Award winners are (whistle) out of the gene pool. But the At Risk Survivors engineer incidents that are not quite fatal—through no fault of the perpetrator! They illustrate the spirit of a Darwin Award candidate. Be careful not to stand too close to an At Risk Survivor!

FAQ: How do you confirm the stories?

The words *Confirmed True by Darwin* indicate that a story is backed up by reputable media sources, or multiple eyewitness accounts. Usually I have read the news report with my own eyes. You can check up on the veracity yourself. Find the story on the Darwin Awards website: Newer stories have a link to media references and the original submission. Search the Slush Pile and the Reject Heap for confirmation. If all else fails, search Google.

www.DarwinAwards.com/book/search.html

All the Darwin Awards and At Risk Survivor stories are believed to be true. None set off my sensitive "Bogus Detector," but sometimes sufficient supporting documentation is lacking. Instead of tossing out a perfectly good escapade, I label these "Unconfirmed." Many a time a reader will e-mail me the confirmation I need. If you know an "Unconfirmed" story is true (or false), *please contact me!*

www.DarwinAwards.com/book/contact.html

When reading the stories, be aware that I do change names and obscure details in the At Risk Survivor stories, in order to provide a measure of anonymity for the innocent—and, for that matter, the guilty. This is to satisfy the legal beagles. Aww, puppies are so cute.

FAQ: Have you ever been wrong?

Once or twice a day! Sometimes I've been spectacularly wrong. The guy who wanted to see what it felt like to be shot with cigarette butts, and was killed by three butts to the heart? I was fooled by bogus media references! It's a hoax, a legend, completely fabricated. It took a *MythBusters* researcher's inquiry for me to realize that I'd been duped! The "urban legend" about the woman who submerged in the ocean to pleasure her man? Oops! Turns out it really happened. The books capture the stories to the best of my current knowledge. The latest scoop is on the continually updated Darwin Awards website.

FAQ: Where do you get your stories?

From you! So keep a sharp lookout in your neighborhood.

Every Darwin Award begins its life as a submission to www.DarwinAwards.com. Nominations come from around the world. Volunteer moderators review the submissions while chanting, "Death. Excellence. Self-selection. Maturity. Veracity." Is it a potential Darwin Award? Is it an At Risk/Near Miss? The best submissions are promoted to the Slush Pile:

www.DarwinAwards.com/slush

Readers rate the Slush Pile stories on a scale from 0 to 10, and I review the Slush Pile stories with the highest vote. Five to ten stories per month strike me as ludicrous enough to be a Darwin Award. I refer to the rules (page 252), moderator comments, and my own intuition when deciding whether a story makes the cut. I rewrite the dry news reports as amusing one-page vignettes, and they go into the permanent archive.

But that's not the end of the process! It's a new beginning. The Darwin Awards website has a vast audience. Approximately one million (1,000,000) visitors read ten million (10,000,000) stories each month. Believe you me, I hear about mistakes. Readers send corrections and confirmations and snarky comments about typos. The Darwin Awards stories are continually updated, and sometimes disqualified, based on community comments.

The stories in this book have been scrutinized, and they are accurate to the best of our knowledge. But due to the dynamic process described above, they are not guaranteed to be entirely accurate. They are a snapshot of the state of human evolution at the time of this writing. As you read the tales contained herein, keep in mind the care with which each gem was culled from dozens of competitors and honed to its current form.

Your vote counts! Visit us at:

www.DarwinAwards.com/slush

FAQ: How many submissions do you get?

Monthly Submissions and Slush Pile Stories

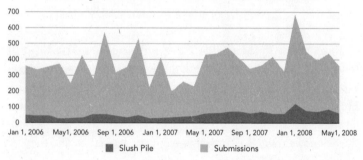

We get two hundred to four hundred submissions per month. About forty go into the Slush Pile, and I pick fewer than ten per month to write into vignettes for the archive.

A particularly sensational story is often submitted hundreds of times. The most recent avalanche was in April 2008: A priest went aloft in a lawn chair tethered to hundreds of helium-filled balloons, à la Lawn Chair Larry. He has not been seen since. As the joke goes, he "ascended to heaven."

Another popular incident happened in May 2005. Two Star Wars acolytes constructed realistic "lightsabers" by filling fluorescent tubes with gasoline and lighting them. They survived (page 197) through no fault of their own!

FAQ: What is the History of the Darwin Awards?

The origin of the first Darwin Award is obscure.

Did the collective processing power of connected computers that formed the early Internet give rise to an electronic consciousness, and were the Darwin Awards this artificial life-form's first attempt at humor? Less fanciful information recently came to light.

Google's Usenet archive contains the oldest known citation, an August 1985 mention of the fellow who crushed himself beneath a Coke machine while trying to shake loose a free can—a true story! The second mention, five years later, is the man who strapped a JATO rocket onto his Chevy. The JATO Rocket Car is the most popular Darwin Award of all time—although it is an Urban Legend. The author of that Usenet posting was Paul Vixie.

Greg Lindahl said, "Everybody knows who Paul Vixie is; he maintains BIND, which holds the Internet together." Greg e-mailed Paul, and Paul, a consummate packrat, produced a 1991 e-mail from Charles Haynes. Charles said that he had heard the term from Bob Ayers: "We sit around talking about Darwin Awards after a hard day's rock climbing. I wonder why. . . ."

My involvement with the Darwin Awards began in 1993. The tongue-in-cheek poke at human evolution tickled my scientific funny bone. I wanted more! Sadly, I could only find five, and tracing the Darwin Awards to their lair proved fruitless. So I began writing new vignettes for my website. I sent out newsletters, encouraged submissions, discussions, and voting. My hobby became a consuming passion. I assumed the alter ego "Darwin" and debated philosophy with readers. These conversations led to the refinement of the concept of a Darwin Award.

I let the Darwin Awards grow under the guidance of my audience. I pruned stories when they told me my judgment was flawed; for instance, if the deceased was the victim of a bizarre accident rather than his own poor judgment. We argued fine points such as whether offspring or advanced age rule out a candidate. And through the years I protected my audience from submissions that would make a hardened criminal cringe.

I said "No!" to pictures of gory accidents, pitiful tales of impoverished people, politically biased stories, racial stereotypes, and just plain mean submissions.

And I deal with flames sympathetically. When community or family members write, I respectfully listen to their point of view. Our discussions sometimes lead to a story being removed. Other times, the family realizes that they can take solace from knowing that their loss might help others avoid the same mistake, if it is used as a "safety lesson" by the Darwin Awards.

The heart and soul of the Darwin Awards is on the Internet. All the stories are available on the website, updated with facts and comments from readers. The Slush Pile is brimming with new submissions. My goal is to maintain a network of people who love the Darwin Awards, and keep this cultural icon true to its origins.

FAQ: What is evolution?

Four attributes cause a species to evolve. (1) The species must show variation. (2) That variation must be inheritable. (3) Not all members of the population survive to reproduce, but (4) the inherited characteristics of some members make them more likely to do so.

FAQ: Are humans really evolving?

Yes! Evolution is the process of a species changing over time to better survive in its environment. The mechanism of evolution is simplicity itself: "Survival of the fittest." A species improves gradually over thousands of generations because of differences in individual rates of reproduction. Evolution eliminates the dodo who does not avoid the club. It eliminates the driver who weaves around on the freeway while yakking on a cell phone. Humans who beget children have their genes represented in the next generation. Those who do not survive to reproduce—do not.

Whether the Darwin Awards represent human evolution is less clear. Is there really a set of genes that causes a man to strap a mortar firework onto his football helmet (page 206)? Do genes really play a role in deciding to kiss a shark (page 244)? These decisions do not have a direct genetic link.

But if a person does not survive to leave offspring, then she is manifestly less fit to survive than the rest of us. Her genes are not part of the next generation. And we can only hope that the next generation will no longer find people jumping into bear cages (page 223), surfing into storm drains (page 31), or whacking bugs with artillery shells (page 175).

Keep in mind that the Darwin Awards also illustrate the creativity that distinguishes us from less adaptable species. The same innovative spirit that causes the downfall of a Darwin Award winner is also responsible for the social and scientific advances that make the human race great.

FAQ: Why aren't the winners those with the highest votes!?

If votes were all that mattered, you would see many more stories about testicles and sex. Put one or both of these in a story, and its score goes up. Grotesque or especially painful stories also get an artificial boost. Ewww! I let the popular vote guide my preference—but not rule it.

The vote *does* overrule my opinion if I love a story that has a low score. For instance, a California man working on his laptop while driving drifted over the centerline and was killed. Ha ha! Ha. Bafflingly unpopular! I rewrote the story more than once, trying to convey the humor I saw, but still I laughed alone. Its score remained low, perhaps because minor injuries were suffered by people in the car he hit. In the end, I heed the conscience of my readers and remove unpopular stories.

FAQ: Would you explain the categories?

There are two categories: the Darwin Award and the At Risk Survivor. Darwin Awards are given to those who can no longer reproduce. At Risk Survivors are just that: people who narrowly escaped a Darwin Award. Many of these are personal accounts, and they are some of my favorites. A near-death experience, written by the self-same idiot who planned it and survived it, certainly serves as a sobering cautionary tale! Most events are confirmed by news reports; some are plausible eyewitness accounts lacking solid confirmation. Unconfirmed Darwin Awards and At Risk Survivors are clearly labeled.

My previous four-category organization caused confusion. There were Darwin Awards, Honorable Mentions, Personal Accounts, and Urban Legends. Each story was either confirmed or unconfirmed. Honorable Mentions were near misses, but even longtime readers often assumed that they were less astounding Darwin Awards. Personal Accounts sometimes were confirmed by news reports or eyewitnesses, causing them to overlap with both Darwin Awards and Honorable Mentions. Urban Legends elicited unfounded scuttlebut regarding the veracity of the Darwin Awards. New legends are scarce now anyway, so the category had languished. The situation is much clearer with only two categories.

FAQ: MEN, Men, men, why so many men?

Nearly all Darwin Award nominees are male. I am aware that males are responsible for aggressive and irrational phenomena like wars, organized religion, drunken driving, et cetera, but pure statistics lead me to believe that more females should be candidates. Is a feminist conspiracy at work in the selection of the candidates?

—*Concerned Reader*

I call 'em as I see 'em. I choose as many women as I can—but I can't use material I don't have. Most of the idiots nominated for this ignominious award are male.

Women are far more likely to be At Risk Survivors than Darwin Award winners, and many of the incidents involving a woman also involve a man. It's difficult to come up with even one chapter per book pertaining exclusively to women. This book has no chapter on women, but the following stories do feature a femme fatale:

MEN, Men, men. Without them, where would we be? Chapterless!

FAQ: Is there an actual physical Darwin Award?

No! Who would I give it to?

This was the #1 question asked by two hundred grammar-school children at my recent book talk. "It would be great if there was an actual Darwin Award!" Recently we began to brainstorm ideas. A herd of sheep on a simple base? A small gray tombstone? R.I.P.

An official certificate? A coffin? A statue of Charles Darwin?

How about a beagle—do you get the reference? Someday there will be an actual, physical Darwin Award that you can give to a boneheaded friend.

FAQ: What are your aspirations?

To be an advisor for *MythBusters'* Darwinian episodes. *MythBusters* rocks! To publish a children's book of the true adventures of Rock, Paper, and Scissors—squirrels I raised from babies to live in the wild. To see my T-shirts, greeting cards, pint glasses, boxers, bumper stickers in stores everywhere! To earn a Ph.D. and become a science writer who is astute and witty enough to fill the shoes of Carl Sagan.

FAQ: Are you making a TV show?

Darwin Awards: The Movie is available on DVD. It was written and directed by Finn Taylor and filmed in the San Francisco Bay Area, using local talent. The movie stars Joseph Fiennes and Winona Ryder. Vignettes include *MythBusters* hosts Jamie and Adam, and the rock band Metallica. This movie is serious silly fun.

Wendy's Movie Vignettes
www.DarwinAwards.com/book/movie.html

Darwin Awards: The Musical, a sensational musical composed by Stephen Witkin, Joey Miller, and Mitch Magonet, is coming to a theatrical stage near you. When Stephen accosted me at a book signing and told me he wanted to write a musical, I reached for the Q-tips. A musical?! But his ideas and script are awesome. Beach Blanket Babylon meets Avenue Q. Great songs have been composed, and the show continues to be developed while seeking Off-Broadway producers.

Darwin Awards: The TV Show. Last but not least, longtime Darwin artist and animator Jay Ziebarth (see his biography on pages 275–276) is working on a TV show animating Darwin Awards vignettes. Stay tuned for more!

FAQ: I saw the Movie. Does it violate the Rules?

Producers assured me that my comments were taken under advisement, which translated into little input on the script. Regrettably, some vignettes in the movie violate the Darwin Awards Rules.

A man accidentally shoots himself while rescuing a friend. That would never become a Darwin Award. People who risk themselves to help others are heroic, not stupid!

An RV is left on autopilot while the driver and passenger entertain themselves in back. The vehicle crashes into a medical building and the result is a bloody dental disaster. Innocent bystanders are injured. That's not allowed in a Darwin Award!

The Coke machine incident—a true event where a man shook a vending machine for a free soda and pulled it over on himself—is transformed into a series of unlikely accidents.

The final word? The movie makes me laugh out loud, even after numerous viewings. Winona's character smokes a joint. An off-screen cameraman dogs the protagonists, citing journalistic integrity at inopportune times. Lawrence Ferlinghetti quietly reads my book in a cameo. A hilarious scene reminiscent of Lawn Chair Larry involves a Mylar balloon. Joseph Fiennes in the shower is a sight not to be missed! The cast and crew put their hearts into the movie. Buy it. Enjoy it.

FAQ: Why do we laugh at stories about death?

Laughter helps us cope with tragedy.

Why are the Darwin Awards funny? My readers are eloquent on the subject.

> "Want to feel like a genius? The next time you feel foolish or incompetent, read a few. You will soon realize how brilliant you really are compared with the morons out there."
>
> "Just makes you feel better about your own intelligence."
>
> "Read these, and a bad day becomes a good one."
>
> "Eventually you die. That's life. And fifty years later you die again because everybody has forgotten you. But if your exit is newsworthy, there's a good chance you will be remembered within your own family, at least. The Darwin Award winners of today will have their memories cherished longer, by more people, than those who die peacefully in bed."
>
> "Whenever I get down on myself, I read one of these and I feel much smarter."

"One truly admires those individuals whose efforts at immortality lift the veil of depression from the rest of us mortals stuck on this rock."

"You think you've got troubles?"

"They make me feel like a genius."

"Anytime I'm feeling down, I read one of these and my life doesn't look so bad anymore!"

I see a little of myself in every story. As one of the world's biggest klutzes my final hour will likely find me clutching a Darwin Award. If so, I know my family and friends will laugh through their tears and say, "That's just like Wendy. Oh, she was such an idiot!"

FAQ: How can I avoid a Darwin Award?

Take a few personal pledges:

"I will keep pointy metal objects away from electrical wires."

"I will not suck bees into a vacuum cleaner."

"I will not disable the safety."

"No rooftop romantic interludes for me!"

Beware the following ideas:

"Instead of following standard procedure . . ."

"Attempting to impress the lady . . ."

"So he could save himself time . . ."

"They tested the ice by jumping up and down."

"A case of beer went into the planning."

"He is still convinced that the toadstool is harmless."
"He refused to let anyone call an ambulance."
"He thought he could outsmart the police."
"The diver had kissed hundreds of sharks."
"He deceived the radiation control supervisor."
"It's a nice snake. Nothing can happen."

Heed good advice:

"Never surf on a flooded street."
"We urge people not to drive with a burning grill in the vehicle."
"The stupidity of cutting through power cables should be obvious."
"Tossing random chemicals down the drain is not wise."
"Only an idiot would jump into the bear cage."

FAQ: Do you drive while using a cell phone?

NO! And you shouldn't either. Humans are not equipped to use these devices safely. Cell phones take too much attention away from input you ought to attend to. Even while walking down the street a person on a cell phone does not notice the needs of others. In the supermarket you will not realize that you are causing an aisle congestion. In a car you will drive slower and more erratically.

I have made changes in my life due to reading thousands of Darwin Awards submissions. One change was no longer using a chair with wheels to reach a high place. The hardest change was to stay off my cell phone while driving.

I did it. You can do it. Get off the phone! **Save a life.**

FAQ: What is with the science essays?

I'm a scientist. I like science! The Darwin Awards are based on the scientific premise that humans are still evolving. Fans often write serious technical dissections of individual stories. A large portion of my readers are college students, or first heard about the Darwin Awards while in college. The science essays are relevant and keep me interested in the job. Charles Darwin would be disappointed in me if I focused only on humor and didn't contribute to scientific knowledge!

FAQ: What do the families think? Do you get their permission?

How awkward would that be?!

If a family writes to me, I take their concerns seriously. Sometimes I remove the story. I don't want to cause anyone pain. Sometimes the family realizes that death has more meaning if it serves as a cautionary tale and saves someone else's life. Often they confide more stupid things that the winner did, prior to his death. Like an Irish wake, it can be healing to laugh while you grieve. That's human nature.

From a recent e-mail: "Many years ago my two uncles started roughhousing at our Christmas gathering. At one point Uncle Frank picked up Uncle John by the heels, lost his grip, and dropped Uncle John on his head. It was all right because John was a state supreme court justice and there for life. The other uncle is, I am sure, in your archive. The one about the skydiving photographer who forgot to put on a chute . . . ?"

FAQ: What inspired you to do this?

Waiting for my science experiments to run their courses was at times tedious. Lee Kozar taught me how to make a website by viewing the source of other web pages and copying the HTML. The Internet was young then, and changing quickly. Boredom was the driving force behind my website, which included personal vignettes as well as the Darwin Awards.

Boredom: the underappreciated motivator.

FAQ: How many stories? How many books? How many more?

In your hands you hold the fifth book.

In June 2008 there were 750 stories on the website. About 600 have been published in five books in twenty-three languages. I will keep writing stories as long as there are stories to write! Or my fingers fall off. Or I win a Darwin Award myself.

FAQ: What is your favorite story?

ABOUT THE DARWIN AWARDS WEBSITE

The Darwin Awards archive was born on a Stanford University web-server in 1994. Its cynical view of the human species made it a favorite subject of conversation in classrooms, offices, and pubs around the world. News of the website spread by word of mouth, and submissions flew in from far and wide. As the archive grew, so did its acclaim.

The website matriculated to its own domain in 1997, won dozens of Internet awards, and now ranks among the top three thousand most-visited websites. It currently entertains a million visitors per month in its comfortable Silicon Valley home. Guests are welcome to set off fireworks and bounce on the trampoline.

The locus of the Darwin Awards community is www.Darwin Awards.com. New accounts of terminal stupidity appear daily in the public Slush Pile. Visitors can vote on stories, sign up for a free e-mail newsletter, and share their opinions on the Philosophy Forum—a community of free thinkers who enjoy philosophical, political, and scientific conversations.

ARTIST BIOGRAPHIES

Pete McDonnell (www.mcdonnellillustration.com) is a freelance illustrator/cartoonist who has created advertising and editorial art for many clients: Microsoft, Southwest Airlines' *Spirit* magazine, Cisco Systems, *National Geographic Kids* magazine, *The Washington Post,* The History Channel, Neiman Marcus, *Sports Illustrated Kids* magazine, Green Giant, Dark Horse Comics, Benefit Cosmetics, *Cracked* magazine, and many others.

He also illustrated *The Darwin Awards: Intelligent Design,* published in 2006. He lives in a small town in northern California with his wife and irrepressible young son.

Jay Ziebarth is an Internet cartoonist, award-winning flash/web designer, TV star, and college dropout. His work has been featured in books, calendars, and greeting cards; it has also circled the globe via his popular cartoon website, zeebarf.com. Jay cocreated the Gemini Award–winning Canadian animated TV series *Sons of*

Butcher. In addition to being the lead character designer, he also starred in the series, which currently airs in 150 countries.

Jay resides in Hamilton, Ontario, with his wife and cat, where he creates dazzling web games and rarely leaves his office.

ABOUT WENDY NORTHCUTT

Wendy studied molecular biology at Berkeley, worked in a neuro-science research laboratory at Stanford, and later joined a biotech start-up developing treatments for cancer and diabetes. She wrote the Darwin Awards while waiting for her dastardly genetic manipulations to yield results.

Eventually Wendy shrugged aside the lab coat in favor of an off-beat career. She now writes both code and prose for the Darwin Awards website. Much of her time is spent wishing she could catch up. In her free time, Wendy chases eclipses, dines, dances, and inhabits an increasingly eccentric wardrobe. Her interests include reading, cats, gardening, glassblowing, natural dyework, fondling textiles, and observing human nature.

Story Index